Free-Heel Boarding

Olivier Couvreur

Title: Free-Heel Boarding

Subtitle: The Techniques and Unique Aspects of Free-Heel Boarding

Author: Couvreur, Olivier

Summary: An introduction to free-heel boarding, the unique Nordic boarding snowsport. Various free-heel boarding techniques are described.

Keywords: snowsports, free-heel, board, ski, Telemark, skwal, monoski, Nordic, Teleboard

Copyright © 2015, 2016 by Olivier Couvreur

All rights reserved. No part of this book may be reproduced or utilized in any form or by any means, electronic or mechanical, including photocopying, recording, or by any information storage or retrieval system, without permission from the author.

Publisher: Olivier Couvreur, Paris XIV, France

Printed by CreateSpace (USA)

Dépôt légal Octobre 2016

ISBN-13: 978-2-9553579-1-0

ISBN-10: 295535791X

Available from Amazon.com and other book stores.

www.free-heel-boarding.com

Free-Heel Boarding

The Techniques and Unique Aspects of Free-Heel Boarding

Olivier Couvreur

www.free-heel-boarding.com

Acknowledgments

I would like to thank the people who took time to review the first version of this book:

Erik Fey, creator of the Teleboard

Thias Balmain, creator of the Skwal, author of *The Inner Glide: The Tao of Skiing, Snowboarding, and Skwalling*

Cindy Kleh, author of *Being a Snowboarder*

This book is dedicated to Sylvia, Alexandra and Viorica. Thank you for your patience when I am out in the mountains.

Contents

Introduction 7
   I am committed free-heeler, but not exclusively. 7
   The origin of this book 9
   Who is this book for? 10
   What is in this book? 10

What is Free-Heel Boarding? 13
   Attempting a definition: gear or technique? 13
   Free-Heel Boarding compared to other downhill skiing sports 15
   The main characteristics of Free-Heel Boarding 18
      Binding positioning 18
      Pole usage 22
      Alpine or Nordic? 23
   Origins of Free-Heel Boarding 24

Why Free-Heel Boarding? 27
   Why do you do that? 27
   Gear specifics: introducing new possibilities 28
   Riding capabilities unleashed - The power of Free-Heel Boarding 36

Free-heel boards & gear 39
   Boards 39
   Bindings and boots 42
   Poles 44
   Protective gear 45

- Free-Heel Boarding techniques 49
  - Stance 49
    - Symmetrical or asymmetrical? 49
    - Standing: basic position 50
    - Riding positions 54
  - Movement 61
    - Basics of skiing mechanics 61
    - Skidding on a free-heel board 63
    - Driving the turn: the figure-8 movement 66
    - The figure-8 movement on a free-heel board 68
    - Jump turns 72
    - Carving low 74
    - Jumping 78
  - Snow conditions 79
    - Powder 79
    - Crud 81
    - Slush 82
    - Bumps / Moguls 84
    - The steeps 86
- Aesthetics and Free-Heel Boarding 89
- Conclusion 97
- Bibliography 98

Introduction

I am committed free-heeler, but not exclusively.

I am a free-heeler. With a background in alpine skiing, I started Telemark skiing in the 1990s. Initially, I wore leather boots on long (195 cm) skis, rented from the only shop in the valley that even had any Telemark gear. Then in 2000, I bought my first pair of Telemark skis and plastic boots.

Later on, I added another dimension to my skiing with free-heel boarding. In the beginning, I practiced free-heel boarding mainly to take a rest from my Telemark days. Committing to Telemarking for a whole day was burning out my legs! However, if I didn't Telemark the entire day, there was still leg muscles left for a few hours of free-heel boarding.

A few years later, I fully expanded my range of snowsports, first, by learning to alpine snowboard, then later, by conquering a skwal and a monoski. While learning to skwal and monoski, I still continued to free-heel board and Telemark ski. I followed the evolution of free-heel gear from leather to plastic; from touring-oriented plastic boots to stiffer gear; and then from 75mm to NTN[1]. At the same time, I added a set of Nordic touring skis to my snowsports quiver (mounted, of course, with Telemark bindings and boots).

---

[1] New Telemark Norm (NTN): In 2007 Rottefella introduced the New Telemark Norm binding. The system's objective is to provide a free-heel Telemark ski binding featuring lateral release, increased lateral rigidity and free-pivot touring functionality.

Introduction

Free-heel skis quiver

The route I followed while learning these various snowsports has made me well aware of the potential for blending the different sports. What you can learn or feel on one type of board can sometime help you progress on another one.

Also, it made me realize that *free-heel boarding is definitely a sport of its own*, with techniques that are specific to the sport. These techniques are very versatile, as is the associated gear, with a wide range of applications and results on all slope conditions.

The origin of this book

Winter is too short ... and spring, summer, and autumn are too long.

This book initially started as a pile of notes written at the end of each ski season. I was in the process of learning some additional alpine snowsports, and still trying to improve on the Nordic ones. At the end of each ski season, I would take notes on where I stood in the learning process and on what the next steps were to improve my technique for the next winter. I assembled a few notes on free-heel techniques, and complemented them with introductory materials to come up with this book.

I have read books on skiing techniques with great interest, and found some useful tips in them. Currently, there is not a single publication available about free-heel boarding; I thought that what I have learned over the last 15 years on free-heel boards might be of interest to others.

I am not a ski instructor or mountain guide, so please forgive my technical approximations. I am not pretending to give a full methodology for learning free-heel boarding from scratch. It is rather a review of the range of applicable free-heel boarding techniques.

Who is this book for?

I hope this book will be useful to skiers of all horizons who want to start free-heel boarding. It aims to show all types of skiers that free-heel boarding is in a unique category of its own within the downhill snowsports family. I want to show the types of maneuvers that are possible with a free-heel board ... and to encourage you to give the sport a try.

This book is also intended to be a starting point for the enhancement of free-heel boarding techniques. I welcome experienced free-heel boarders around the world to respond and provide their own views on free-heel boarding. As there are multiple approaches to free-heel skiing, there might also be to free-heel boarding.

What is in this book?

This book is an essay on free-heel boarding as a sport rather than a full methodological guide. I assume that each reader is proficient in at least one other downhill snowsport, such as skiing, snowboarding, free-heel skiing, skwalling or monoskiing. Therefore, the basic aspects common to all these sports won't be addressed here.

I discuss the state of free-heel boarding today and how it fits in as a downhill skiing sport. I also discuss the paradox of free-heel boarding in greater depth, and how free heels (an apparently odd set-up on a board) can turn a single board into a versatile and efficient gliding tool. Then, I examine some technical elements of free-heel boarding, followed by a consideration of some of the sport's aesthetic qualities.

What is Free-Heel Boarding?

Attempting a definition: gear or technique?

Free-heel boarding can simply be defined as skiing downhill on a single board mounted with free-heel bindings. One foot is in front of the other along the longitudinal axis of the board. The angle between the axis of the board and the axes of the bindings is relatively low.[2]

This introductory definition raises a question: Can free-heel boarding be defined exclusively as the usage of a specific combination of boots, bindings, and board?

A parallel can be drawn by defining Telemark skiing. Telemark is a technique of turns performed on free-heel skis, but using free-heel skis does not necessarily imply Telemarking. Free-heel skis can also

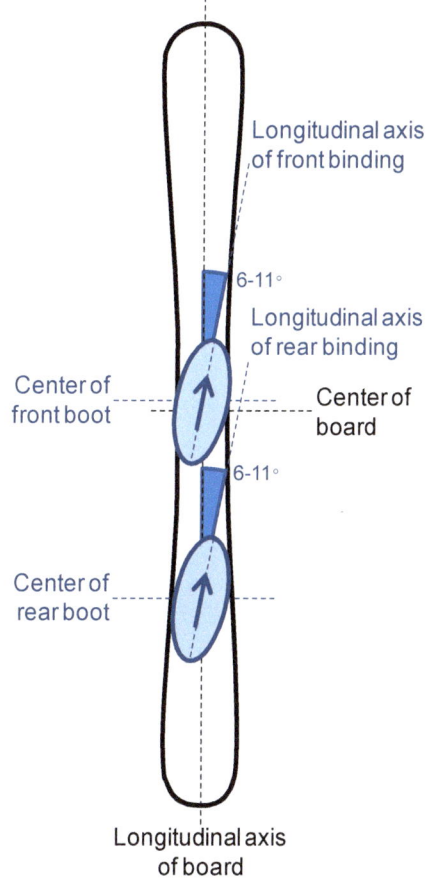

---

[2] Between 6° and 11°; even if a range from 1° to 35° is mentioned in the Nordic skiboard patent.

be used to do parallel-alpine turns.

When applying parallel techniques, of course, some specifics of the gear used have to be taken into account (for example, not putting too much weight on the front of the cuff of the front boot). Parallel techniques are efficient and relevant even with free-heel skis, but they do not use the full potential of the free heel; whereas, the free-heel aspect is at the center of the Telemark technique.

So is it for free-heel boarding. Using a board mounted with free-heel bindings can be done relying solely on techniques borrowed either from the skwal or monoski.

So, just as *Telemark* techniques can only be used on free-heel skis, there is a specific set of *free-heel boarding* techniques that can only be used on a free-heel board. On the other hand, there are many techniques that can be used on free-heel boards, including some that do not fully use all of the free-heel benefits.

In this book, I cover *free-heel boarding* techniques as well as other sets of relevant techniques that can be used on free-heel boards, paying particular attention to their adaptation to this unique set of gear.

Therefore, I would define *free-heel boarding* as a set of techniques for skiing downhill on a single board mounted with free-heel bindings.

This book encompasses:

1) A core of techniques only applicable to free-heel boards.

2) A wealth of other techniques that originated in other types of gear, but are adaptable to free-heel gear.

Free-Heel Boarding compared to other downhill skiing sports

Subfamilies of downhill skiing sports can be defined by their association with a specific snow-device (one board or two skis) and a specific interface (binding and boot) for firmly connecting this device to the rider. Seven major downhill snow sports can be identified:

- Alpine skiing
- Free-heel skiing
- Alpine snowboarding
- Soft-boot snowboarding
- Monoskiing
- Skwalling
- Free-heel boarding

Within these sports listed above are inner variations of styles and purposes, for which there are specific characteristics in the boards, bindings, and boots.

Characteristics	Alpine skis	Free-heel skis	Alpine Snowboard	Soft-boot snowboard	Monoski / Monoboard	Skwal	Free-Heel board
1 / 2 boards	2 skis	2 skis	1 board	1 board	1 board	1 board	1 board
Bindings	Alpine bindings	Free-Heel bindings	Plate bindings	Strap-in, step-in bindings	Alpine / plate bindings[1]	Plate bindings	Free-Heel bindings
Binding positioning	On longitudinal axis of each ski	On longitudinal axis of each ski	Max +40° (for front) away from longitudinal axis	Perpendicular to the longitudinal axis of the board: (+/-25° away of perpendicular axis)	Next to each other, parallel to the longitudinal axis of the board	In front of each other Max +10° away from longitudinal axis[2]	In front of each other Max +15° away from longitudinal axis[3]
Boots	Hard-shell ski boots	Hard-shell boots with bellows	Hard-shell boots	Soft-shell boots	Hard-shell boots	Hard-shell boots	Hard-shell boots with bellows
Pole usage	Yes, part of the technique	Yes, part of the technique	No, never	No, never	Yes, part of the technique	Eventually, for specific snow conditions	Yes, commonly used but usage can be limited to specific snow conditions[4]
Family	Alpine	Nordic	Alpine	Alpine	Alpine	Alpine	Nordic

[1] In the case of monoski, I am not distinguishing between traditional alpine skiing bindings and plate bindings or between types of boards. In fact, the difference from traditional monoskiing and monoboarding is more a matter of board characteristics and style.
[2] On a skwal, the front binding can even be set to 0° or with a slight negative angle such as -1°.
[3] I'll discuss the angle of bindings in the gear section of this book. For classification purposes, the key point is that in free-heel boarding, the bindings are globally aligned with the longitudinal axis of the board, but not as much as on a skwal.
[4] Regarding pole usage, I am trying to stay synthetic. One should basically distinguish between their most common use today among the riders and their role in the skiing technique, to be precise, and analyze this aspect. I am trying to keep it simple in this overview table, and therefore will mix both notions.

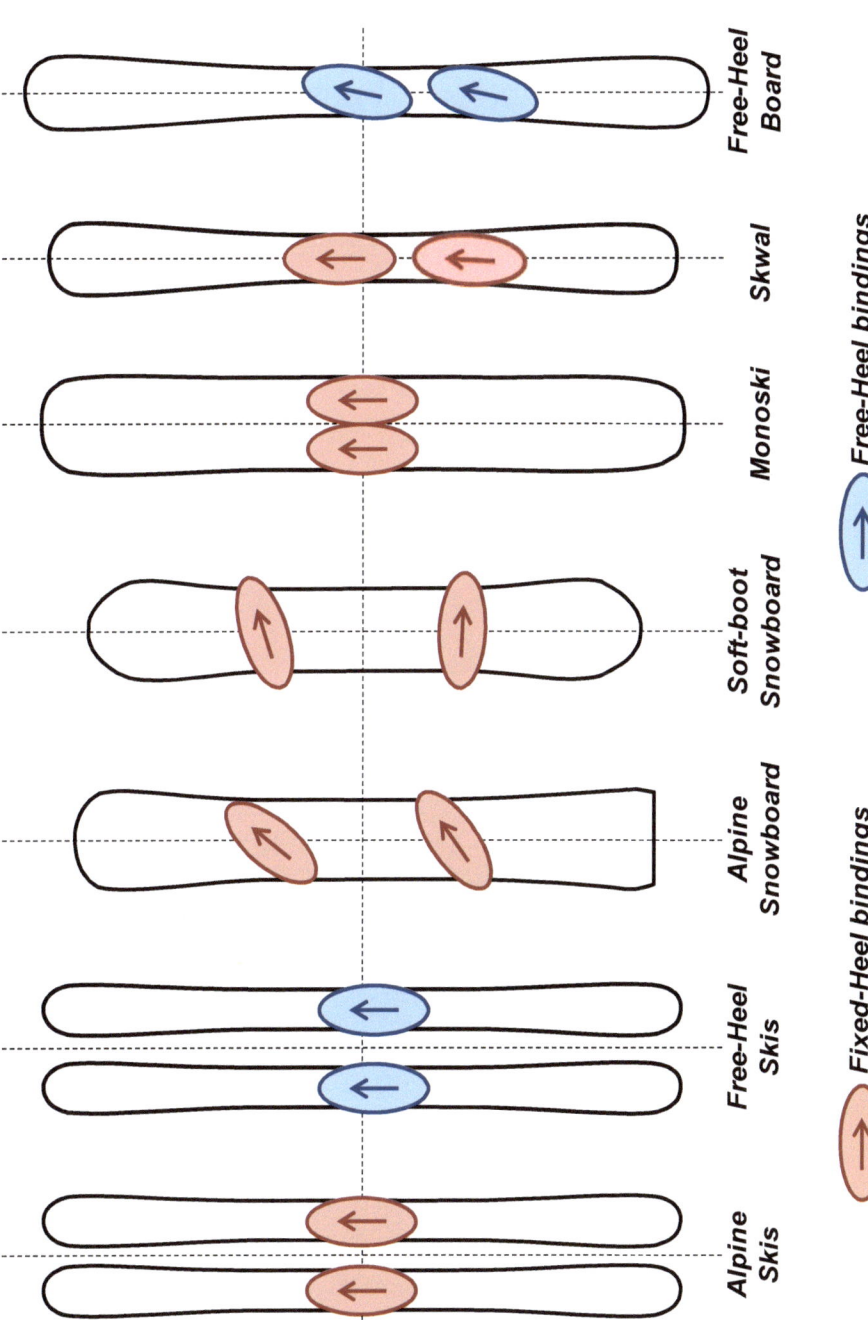

The main characteristics of Free-Heel Boarding

Let's discuss how free-heel boarding is classified in the previous table, with its unique combination of a single board and free-heel bindings.

Binding positioning

The bindings are positioned so that one foot is in front of each other, but with a noticeable angle from the longitudinal axis of the board. There is a limited distance between the two feet; a few centimeters only, just to allow space for the rear binding to fit in. The center of the board is located under the front foot.

Bindings

On currently available boards, the angle is the same for both feet. If the gear would allow for some finer angle adjustment, there would certainly be room for experimentation. However, having both feet at the same angle of around 8-9 degrees is a starting position.

1) A significant positive angle on the rear binding allows you to bring the rear knee to the side of the front knee. Its way forward is not blocked by the front leg. (We'll discuss later how that provides unique possibilities specific to free-heel boarding, and how it also allows using some techniques inherited from monoski.)

2) Having a similar angle on both bindings makes it a little bit easier to stand still (just compare a skwal and a snowboard when not moving); the position is relatively natural, and therefore not too tiring.

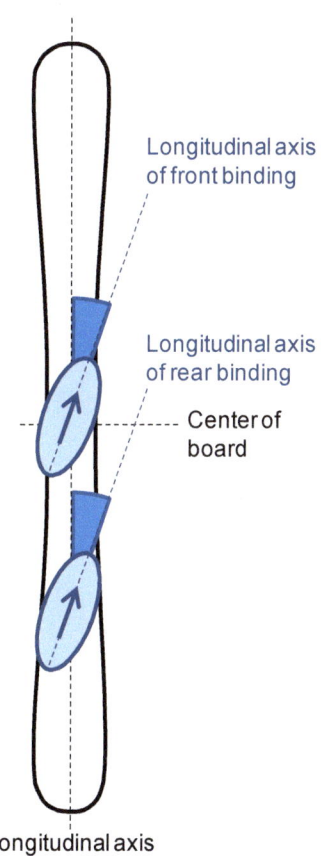

What is Free-Heel Boarding?

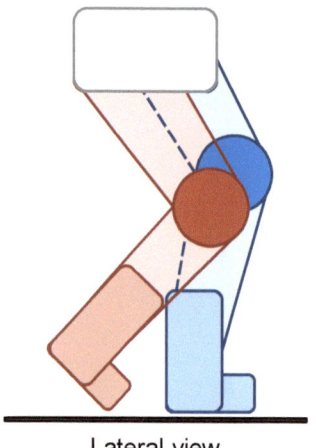

Lateral view

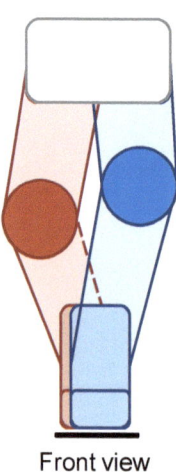

Front view

Let's consider the reasons for moving around these binding positions:

- A smaller angle on the front binding would go against point #2 above, and definitely against #1.

- A wider angle on the front binding would increase the angle on the rear binding too. It would lead to a significantly asymmetrical position; whereas, the front binding needs to stay aligned with the longitudinal axis of the board, as if it were a single Telemark ski.

- A smaller angle on the rear binding goes against point #1, and blocks the movements of the rear leg, possibly reducing significantly the advantages that a free rear heel provides. The binding setup would end up looking like a skwal-like position.

- A wider angle on the rear binding (without changing anything on the front one) might provide a more stable equilibrium at low speeds. However, a wider angle goes against point #2, and leads to a loss of control on movements perpendicular to the board (as the rear binding and boot allows some bending in that direction).

So, an efficient binding setup for free-heel boarding is generally defined by:

- both binding axes close to the longitudinal axis of the boards;

- a slightly positive angle on the rear binding, which should be wide enough to allow the rear knee to come forward next to the front knee (not *in* the front knee). It should, however, not be too wide, so that it keeps good lateral force transfer capabilities.

The width of the board is designed so that the fronts of the feet are close to one edge, and the backs of the feet are close to the other edge.

Pole usage

Most of the time, free-heel boarders are seen with a pair of ski poles. Poles are, indeed, very convenient for not wasting energy while you are standing, or for going through challenging terrains such as moguls, steeps, etc.

In fact, the use of poles in free-heel boarding is simply pragmatic. They are convenient and useful, and so are part of the free-heel boarder's equipment. However, they are not always used.

Using poles

Alpine or Nordic?

Classifying free-heel boarding in one family or the other is not an obvious task.

With a free-heel board fully attached to your feet, you only have one way to go – downhill, just as it is with any other board (beside split boards). And there are no obvious limitations in attacking steep slopes. Just like any other board, free-heel boarding has roots in the alpine family of skiing techniques.

Some define the Nordic family of skiing techniques as everything with a free-heel. It therefore encompasses Telemark, Randonnée/Nordic touring, and cross-country skiing. Under this definition, free-heel boarding would be a Nordic technique. But Nordic techniques come from regions where skis were used as means of daily transport, so this does not apply to free-heel boards.

I am clearly opting to join the Nordic family, because:

- Most of today's free-heel boarders come from free-heel skiing.
- The only boards produced today for this dedicated purpose are Teleboards. The original concept of Teleboard (as patented) was a split *Nordic skiboard* – two free-heel skis that could be used to climb uphill and then turned into a single free-heel board for the descent.

Origins of Free-Heel Boarding

It's hard to say who invented free-heel boarding. Free-heel set-ups on a single ski were reported in Sweden and France, but the idea certainly emerged in more than one brain. A few experimented with the idea. Some prototypes, including very odd-looking ones, have certainly been tried here or there.

However the first to register a patent that included the idea of a free-heel board were Martin Fey, Erik Fey and Marie Franzino from United States in 1998. The Fey brothers were also the first to launch a production of boards dedicated to free-heel boarding with a built-in insert pattern onto which free-heel bindings could be screwed.

Free-heel boarding origins could also be considered under a wider historical perspective. Free-heel boarding is at the confluence of the rebirth of Telemark skiing and the development of boarding snowsports. Free-heel boarding was introduced by free-heel (Telemark) skiers rather than boarders adopting free-heel skiing and techniques.

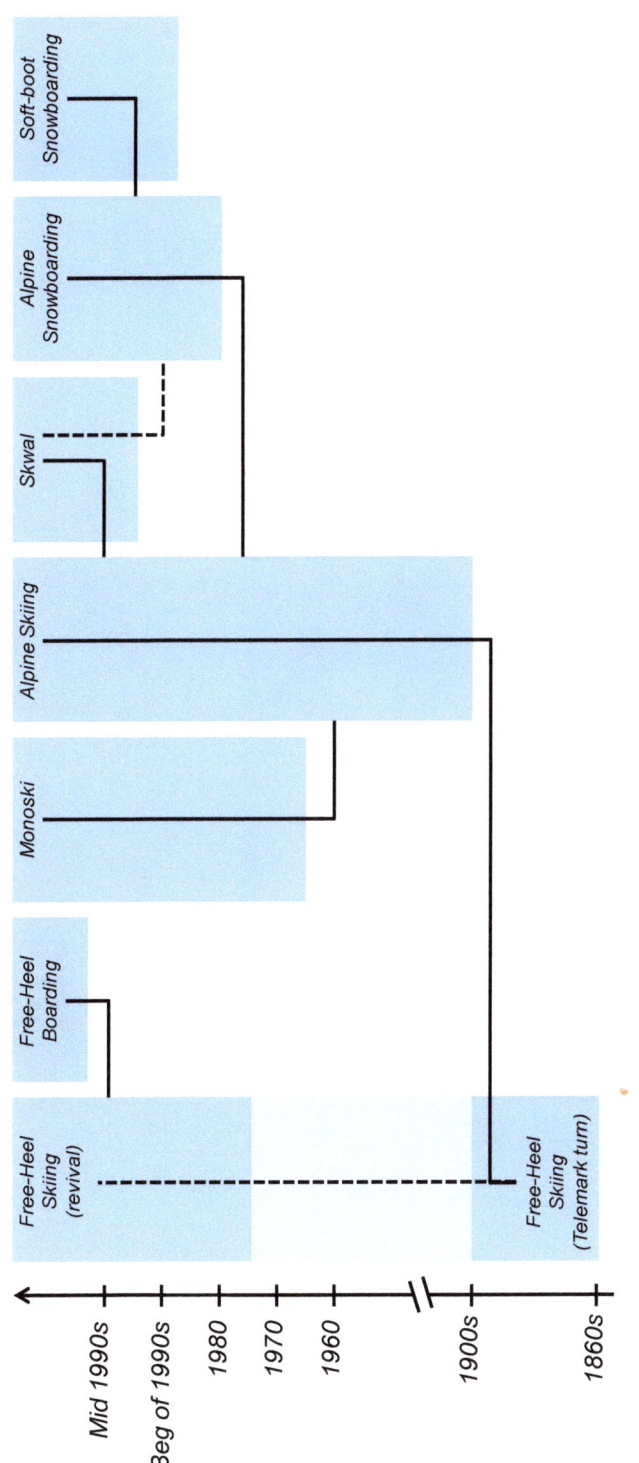

Why Free-Heel Boarding?

Why do you do that?

"What is that? Why do you do that? What's wrong with you?"

Thankfully, that is not the typical reaction of skiers seeing a free-heel boarder for the first time, but it sometimes happens (especially in lift lines … not as much going downhill!). Indeed, if considering just the gear, free-heel boarding is merely the combination of a board and free-heel bindings. So why would one make a skwal (with the closest binding position on a board) less efficient by switching plate bindings for a toe-only binding system? Why would a skier (who is already crazy enough to be using inefficient free-heel bindings, by the way) trade in two skis for one?

That misses the main point of free-heel boarding! *It is a set of techniques of its own.* Of course, if you want fried eggs for breakfast; you'll use a frying pan. If you want a hard-boiled egg, you'll take an egg-boiler or a saucepan full of water. But if you have no idea that fried eggs exist, you won't see the use of the frying pan. And if you know it exists, but want to have a boiled egg anyway, you'll use the saucepan.

When I want to go skwalling, I take a skwal. When I want to go monoskiing, I take a monoski. When I am missing Telemark, I take my free-heel skis. But when I take one of my free-heel boards, it's for cooking up something special!

Free-heel boards exist not just because it is the last possible combination of bindings and boards, and not just for the sake of skiing on something different. **Free-heel boards are used because they deliver something which cannot be found in any other snow sport.**

I will first discuss what the free-heel setup technically allows. Then I will introduce the power potential of free-heel boarding and the possibilities that it can offer.

Gear specifics: introducing new possibilities

Free heels provide more movement options.

As previously mentioned, an efficient binding position for free-heel boarding is globally defined as:

- Both binding axes close to the longitudinal axis of the board.
- A slight positive angle on the rear binding: enough to allow the rear knee to come forward, next to the front knee (not *in* the front knee; but a little more for keeping lateral-force-transfer capabilities).
- A slight positive angle on the front binding to bring the front leg into a natural position with the rear leg as defined above.

This position, as well as having both heels free, will notably allow the free-heel boarder to:

- Bring the rear knee forward, to the side of the front knee.
- Move the rear knee (if regular, the right foot) from far away on the right of the board to a bit left and back of the front knee.
- Get very low with the back knee.

In a nutshell, the back knee can go anywhere it needs.

Why Free-Heel Boarding?

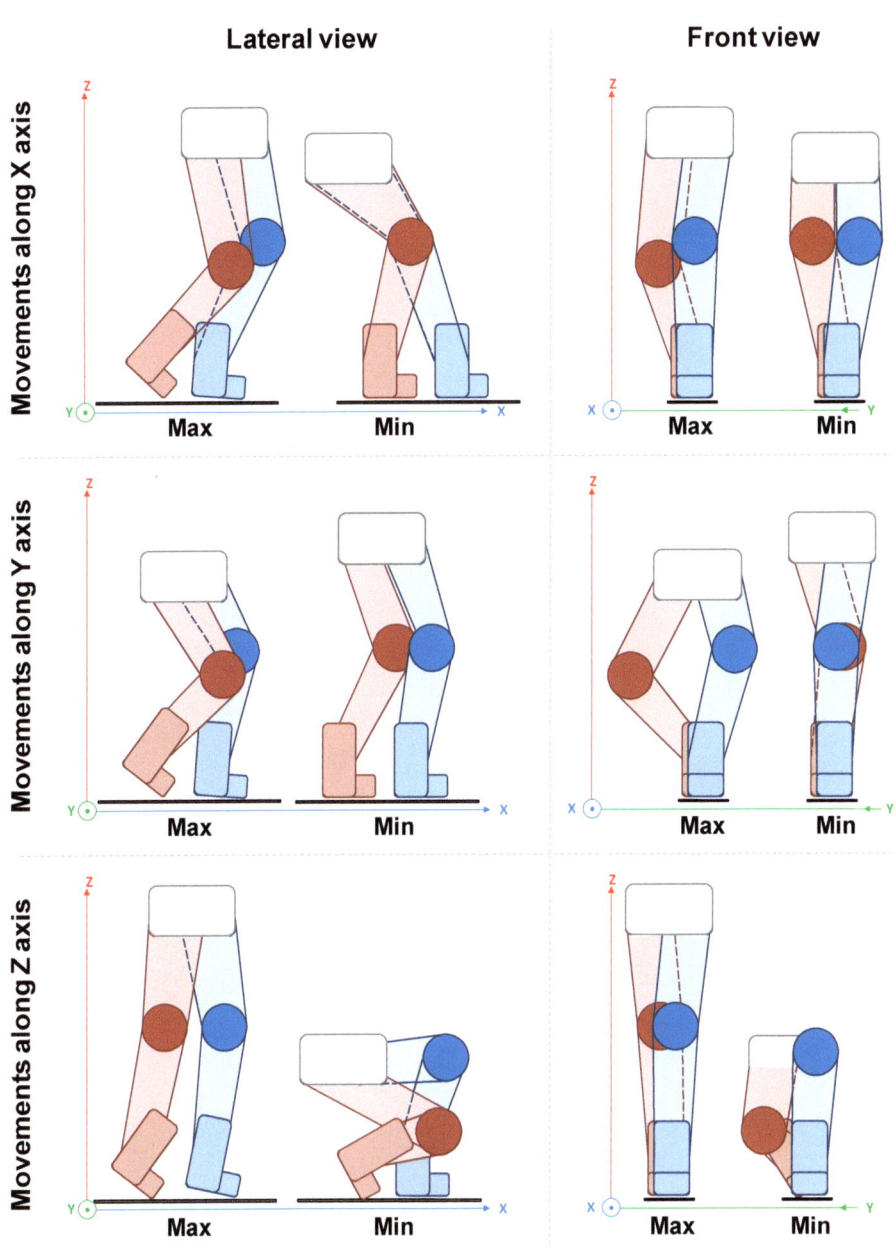

Lateral view

Movements along X axis

Max

Min

Movements along Y axis

Max

Min

Movements along Z axis

Max

Min

Front view

Movements along X axis

Max — Min

Movements along Y axis

Max — Min

Movements along Z axis

Max — Min

In a way very different from all the other boards, free-heel boarding provides opportunities for:

- Influencing the angle of the edge of the board on the snow (rotation around X-axis).

- Quickly and precisely controlling the direction of the board (rotation around Z-axis).

- Independently acting on each foot with very little resistance from the boots/binding in the front/back direction (voluntary, directed rotation around the Y-axis is then possible).

- Absorbing terrain variation (going up and down Z-axis).

- Quickly engaging and disengaging the board in the direction of the movement (going back and forth on the X-axis).

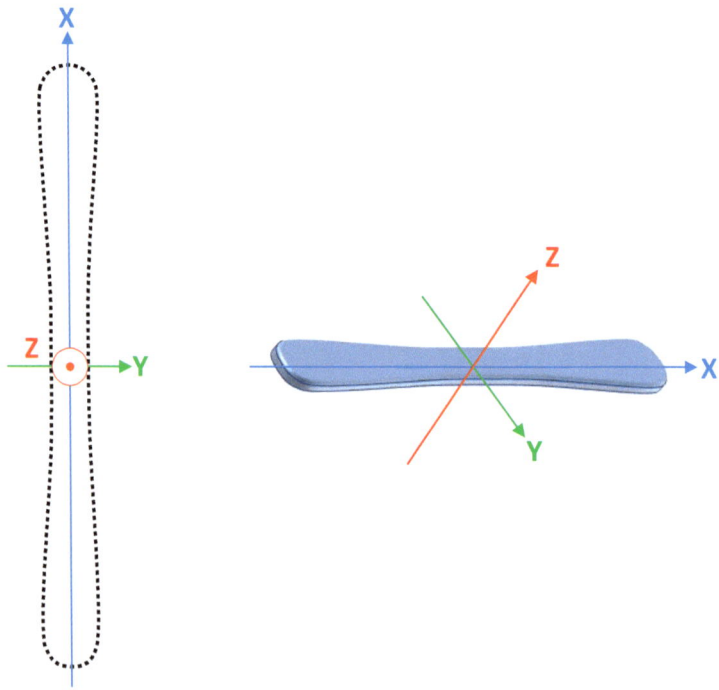

There are no facilitated movements along the Y-axis. The lateral rigidity of the bindings and boots, which are attached to a single rigid board, do not permit this.

The free-heel boarder is not going to rely solely on this to initiate and drive turns. Free-heel boarding is still based on the basics of downhill snow skiing. These extra possibilities of movement offered by free-heel gear add to the classic ski techniques, and help in absorbing different types of terrain variations.

Freedom-of-the-heel also brings some limitations. In the learning process, the first characteristic of free-heel bindings that novice Telemark skiers usually notice is that it allows them to fall forward with their face directly in the snow – without anything holding them back. That cannot happen with a free-heel board. Indeed, both heels are free, but the toes are permanently pointing in the direction of this possible fall. Consequently, the attached back leg keeps the front leg from going all the way down on the front binding, which prevents a forward fall. Thigh strength considerably diminishes, if not eliminates, the risk of a forward fall. The binding positioning completely solves this potential problem.

The binding positioning along the longitudinal axis of the boards brings up another real limitation in comparison to a skwal or a snowboard. The boarder cannot use the rigidity of the boots to bend the board (lateral flex on a snowboard or forward/aft flex on a skwal), nor influence the radius of the turns.

Why Free-Heel Boarding?

A forward-facing stance is a key driver of the development of the free-heel boarding technique.

Free-heel boarding, universally has a front-facing or downhill-facing stance like skiing, monoskiing and skwalling. This stance is *unlike snowboarding*. A forward-facing stance is a key driver of the development of the free-heel boarding technique.

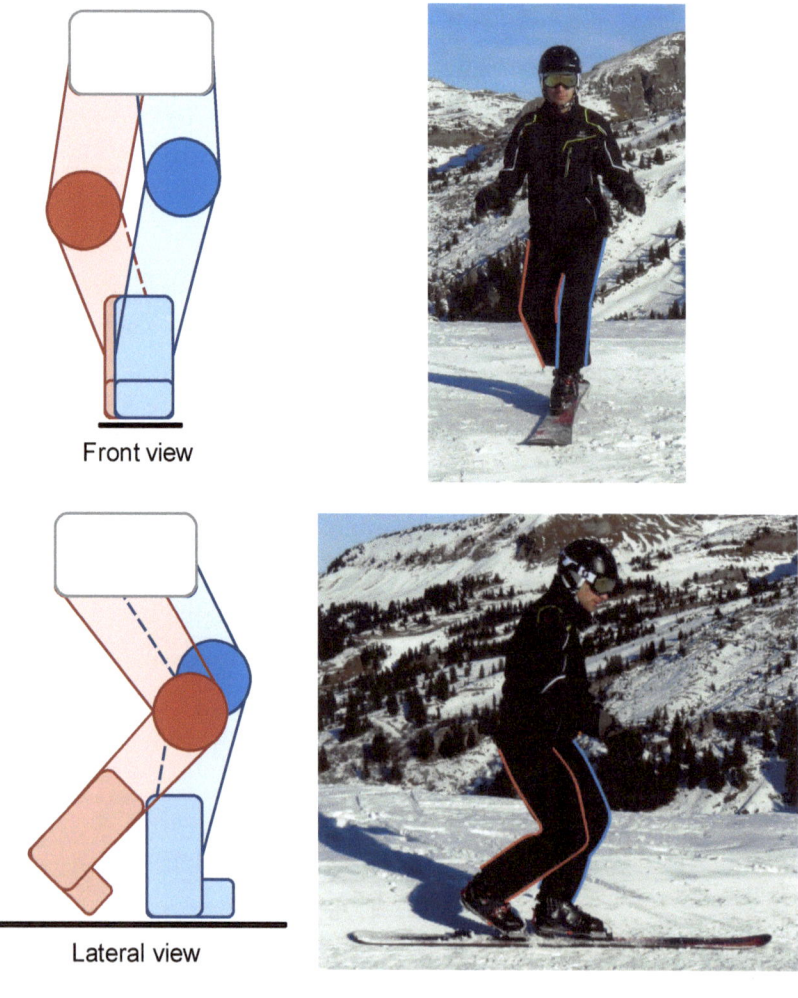

Front view

Lateral view

Pole-usage is pragmatic, and it extends the range of skiable conditions with comfort.

Today's free-heel boarders are usually seen with poles. Poles, indeed, help you conserve energy while you stand and make challenging terrain easier to navigate (such as moguls, steeps, etc.). But honestly, you can also free-heel board without them on all types of terrain. Just look at skwallers!

In fact, the use of poles in free-heel boarding just makes sense. They are convenient and useful, so they are part of the free-heel-boarder equipment. The point is to know when to use them, and when you are better off without them, so you don't overuse them.

This sensible approach to using poles allows you to easily and safely access a wider range of terrain and snow conditions with ease and comfort.

Riding capabilities unleashed - The power of Free-Heel Boarding

The range of possibilities of movement free-heel board gear offers has been discussed. How can we take advantage of these opportunities in the free-heel boarding technique?

The following image is self-explanatory. The free-heel setup provides some interesting advantages for all kinds of snow conditions.

For example, the maneuverability provided by a facilitated rotation around the vertical axis (Z) will enable you to ride long boards (around 2 meters) without any issue. With a longer board, floating capabilities are outstanding (which is great for powder). The stability is very good at any speed, and the effective edge ensures a good grip for some committed carving.

The free knee allows precise and quick controlling of the rotation around the longitudinal axis (X), therefore, adjusting the angle of the edge on snow. This is essential to accurately and efficiently initiate turns.

The wide flexion-extension capabilities along the vertical axis (Z) will be able to absorb various terrain changes well. This can be a very useful feature in many other situations, such as landing jumps. Furthermore, it makes extreme carving push-pull techniques easier.

With a free-heel board, you can make the tip and tail go up and down while keeping your weight in the middle of the board. The board can rotate around the Y-axis independently of your weighting. This will open the way for truly three-dimensional control in powder!

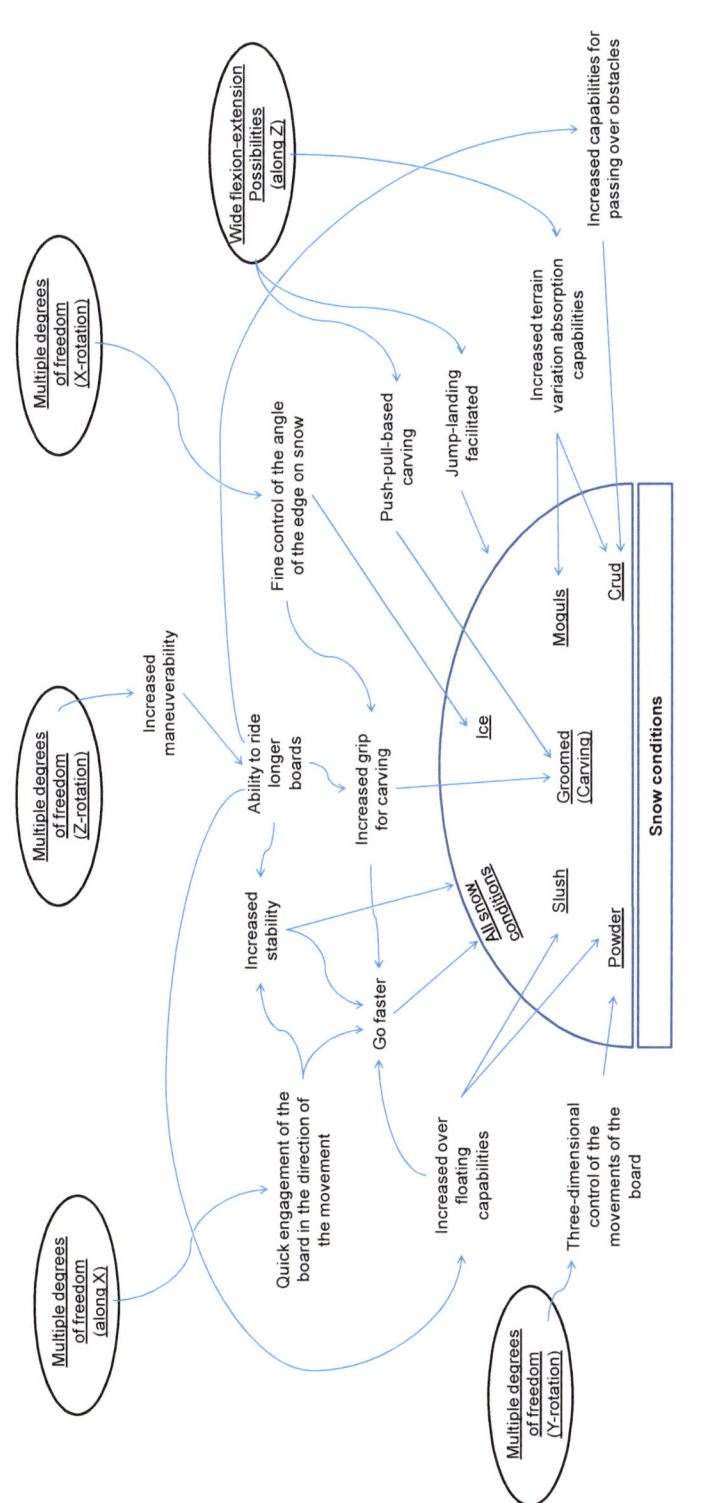

So, at first glance, there is indeed a bit of a paradox with free-heel boards. The combination of free-heel bindings and a single board leads to an apparently odd set-up. But looking at it more carefully, it opens a unique range of possibilities – of movements especially – that can be turned into an advantage in many snow conditions. Freedom-of-the-heel leads directly to less control on the board, but it also provides many possibilities of movement which can be used for more control on multiple axes. In the end, these extra capabilities far exceed the initial loss, in terms of control and versatility.

We now need to use all these possibilities in a coherent free-heel boarding technique, while borrowing technical elements from other sports (monoski, skwal, snowboard) to refine and boost them with the free heel.

Free-heel boards & gear

Boards

As of today, board production dedicated to free-heel boarding is limited to Teleboard®. Therefore, they set the standards for the sport.

Model	186	Pursuit 191	Sheriff 198
Length	186 cm	191 cm	198 cm
Tip	192 mm	199 mm	206 mm
Waist	131 mm	127 mm	137 mm
Tail	180 mm	185 mm	192 mm
Side cut radius		9.3m	

All Teleboard models have a round-shaped tail. Tips are not very high, but benefit from an "early rise" shaping.

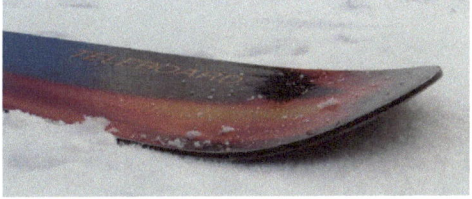

There is also a wide range of boards built for skwalling that can be used as free-heel boards. Their lengths range from 165cm to 195cm and their turning radii range from 8 to 17 m.

Besides the actual dimensions of the board, its stiffness is also important. A board mounted with free-heel bindings cannot be deliberately bent by the boarder. It should, therefore, not be too stiff to bend dynamically during the turn. A wide range of stiffness is possible, however. Stiffness has impact on the board's possible uses. The softer boards will not be as efficient in carving, but they can be very pleasurable to ride.

Indeed, as softer boards bend with less effort, they also rebound the energy of bending more easily and smoothly. In some optimum snow conditions, it feels like the board is driving itself with effortless turning.

Regarding edges, they are present along the whole length of the board. The tuning of edges is a question of feel for each boarder. Sharply tuned edges along the whole length of the board will provide extreme carving advantages. However, with such tuning, the board will be more challenging to ride in conditions that are less than "corduroy," and the turning technique might require some adaptations.

Finally, above the edges, the sidewalls are also an important component of the board. They support intense carving, and should also be a gliding surface.

Bindings and boots

75mm and NTN bindings are two possible options. The NTN binding increases the lateral control considerably and the transmission of power on free-heel skis. That is its main advantage; it has also detractors.

On a free-heel board, due to the position of the legs and the fact that both feet are linked to a single board, NTN bindings do not provide a huge advantage.

NTN and 75mm boots

So both types of bindings can be considered, but NTN is not required for the most intense carving. Also, as in free-heel skiing, 75mm cable bindings allow for the use of softer boots, providing a different feel from the stiffer ones.

In terms of mounting on the board:

- As previously discussed, the angle of the axis of the binding to the longitudinal axis of the board will be between 6 and 11 degrees for both bindings.

- Raised-plate bindings can be used with the same results as on free-heel skis – to improve carving capabilities. Consequently, they are usually mounted on stiffer boards.

Raised-plate bindings

In regards to boots: racing or touring Telemark boots can be used, depending on the board and style of riding. I personally use Scarpa T1 as a racing boot for free-heel boarding, as well as T2 for a softer, more versatile boot.

For the final touch, a single safety leash on the front biding is advisable. It will allow you to get prepared for riding without having to keep a permanent eye on your board.

Poles

Poles used for free-heel boarding are shorter than for Telemark skiing. This is due to the stance, which can be very low. Too-long-of-a-pole would almost require you to have your hand over the head when planting the pole in a low stance.

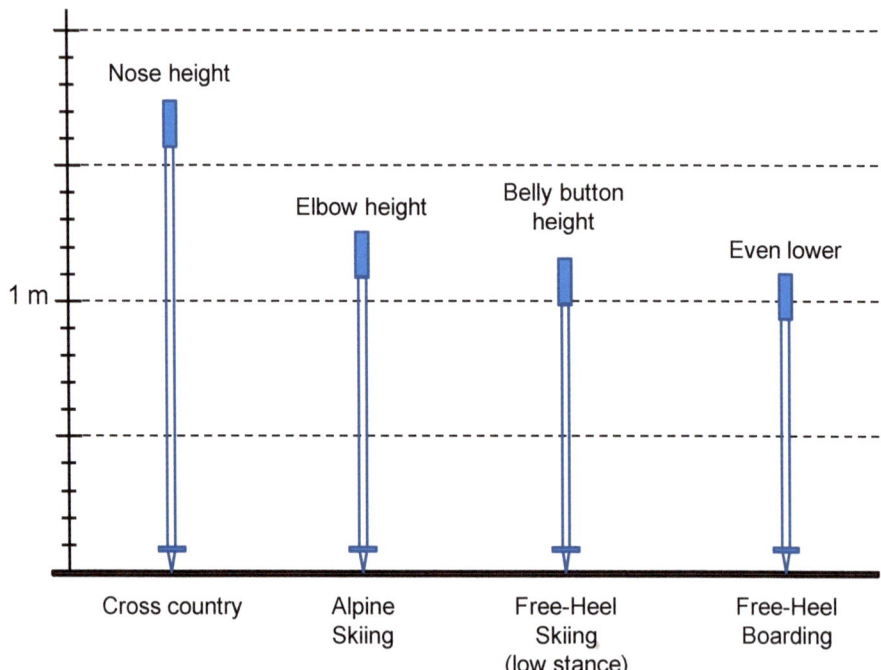

Adjustable-size poles are useful, as they can adapt to all snow conditions. They can be reduced to a very short size, or even folded, and they are convenient to carry in a backpack. That allows for riding without poles, and when snow conditions do require poles, you will have them already on you.

Protective gear

Besides board, bindings, boots and poles, protective gear is also important:

- **Helmet:** A helmet is recommended, as in all high-speed snow sports. A full-face helmet is, of course, more protective, but you are not more likely to fall on your face free-heel boarding compared to other skiing/boarding sports. Despite the free heels, a full fall forward is very uncommon, as the positioning of the legs prevents this type of fall.

- **Backpack/back protector:** Falls on the back in normal conditions are relatively uncommon, as well. Of course, if you go for big air, that's another story. It is always better to wear protection than not. If you are carrying things on your back (e.g. folded poles), a back protector becomes a must-have. One possible option is a backpack with a built-in back protector.

- **Gloves:** Carving with hands in the snow kills the best gloves faster than anything else. Even snowboard gloves that claim to be the most resistant available will not survive real carving for long. These gloves are good enough to be used regularly in the snow, and even dragged in the snow during turns. But with extreme carving, the hands will be fully in the snow with 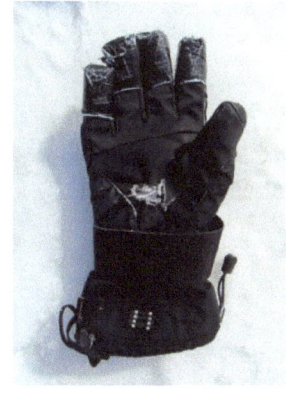 part of the weight of the body on them. If the snow is freshly groomed and slightly refrozen, it is like holding the gloves on a sander machine. The gliding surface of the gloves therefore needs to be reinforced. Multiple layers of Powertape® are a cheap and accessible option. The glove can also be soaked into some chemicals which, when hardened, will be quite resistant to abrasion. A homemade plastic gliding pad can also be used. As for the choice of the glove itself, minimal built-in protection can be safer for carving. Because free-heel boarding is front-facing, the hand contacts the snow near the bottom of the palm. So protection under this part of the hand and wrist is important. It is also sufficient, as the hands still need to be mobile enough to allow for the grabbing of poles.

- **Arm protection:** During an extreme-carved turn, the whole forearm is in the snow with pressure on it. A carving session with a free-heel board can leave some bruises along the forearm. Specific protective surfaces from the palm of the hand to the elbow can be useful for carving if they are designed as a gliding surface that can support these extreme carving turns.

- **Eyewear:** This is your choice, but goggles are handy, as you are often quite close to the snow.

- **Knee pads:** Telemarkers with a low stance uses knee pads to protect themselves from stones or ice hidden in the snow. I do not find them essential on free-heel boards. The front knee does not go in the snow, and is protected by the board. The back knee doesn't wander into the snow as much either as it does on free-heel skis.

Free-Heel Boarding techniques

Stance

Symmetrical or asymmetrical?

The pattern for mounting the bindings on the board is asymmetrical. Having one foot in front of the other creates an asymmetrical position for the boarder, anyway.

On one hand, it does not necessarily make the techniques fully asymmetrical. For the sake of comparison, skwalling – of which free-heel boarding is closely related in terms of binding position – is a front-facing and rather symmetrical technique; whereas snowboarding is clearly asymmetrical. On the other hand, the free heel enables the rear knee to go down, in a position resembling a Telemark turn. This is only possible on one side, making the related technique clearly asymmetrical but still front-facing.

The free-heel boarding technique is somewhere between *symmetrical* and *asymmetrical*. It depends on the subset of techniques considered. Techniques resembling monoskiing and skwalling are rather symmetrical, whereas the core of free-heel boarding techniques (i.e. the one that cannot be linked to the two other disciplines previously mentioned) includes more asymmetrical components.

Consequently, the concepts of *backside* or *frontside* turns are seldom used. Free-heel boarding is definitely *front-facing*. I will mostly speak of rear or back legs, which is enough to discuss the asymmetrical aspects of this discipline.

Standing: basic position

The relaxed stance of a free-heel boarder is characterized as follows:

- Back heel is slightly lifted up.
- Weight is a bit more on the front leg than the rear one.
- The whole upper body is facing the tip of the board.
- The torso is relatively vertical, eventually leaning a little forward.
- Hands are in front of the boarder, elbows bent.

Basic position with poles

Key characteristics of the basic position

Free-Heel Boarding Techniques

Free-heel gear keeps the board centrally weighted when you have a very low stance or a high stance. Free-heel boards can be used with a less-high stance, depending on the boarder. As you gain on speed, you will also generally move more to a lower stance than the relaxed, natural one. This tightly draws the thighs, allowing for both better absorption of terrain variations and more reactivity.

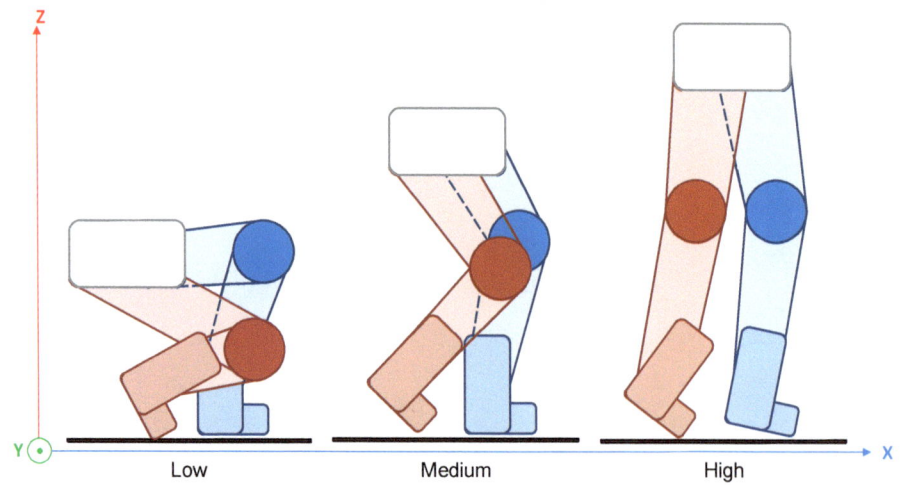

Low — Medium — High

Low — Medium — High

This leads to having relatively low poles (in comparison to skiing or even free-heel skiing). Poles should not be too long, or they cannot be efficiently used on aggressive turns starting from a low position. Even if they are short, the poles are still high enough to be used with a high stance when they are needed to help with balance and rhythm.

When it comes to turning, your weight should not be placed in one direction or another; it is always projected on the feet. This is a very important point, as your center of gravity is the center of the movement.

Riding positions

Three basic positions can be distinguished for riding on a free-heel board:

- The in-**L**ine knee position (L) in which:

    - The back heel will be kept low.

    - The back knee will be positioned slightly behind the front knee.

    - The space between the front of the back knee and the back of the front knee is very limited; they will touch each other from time to time.

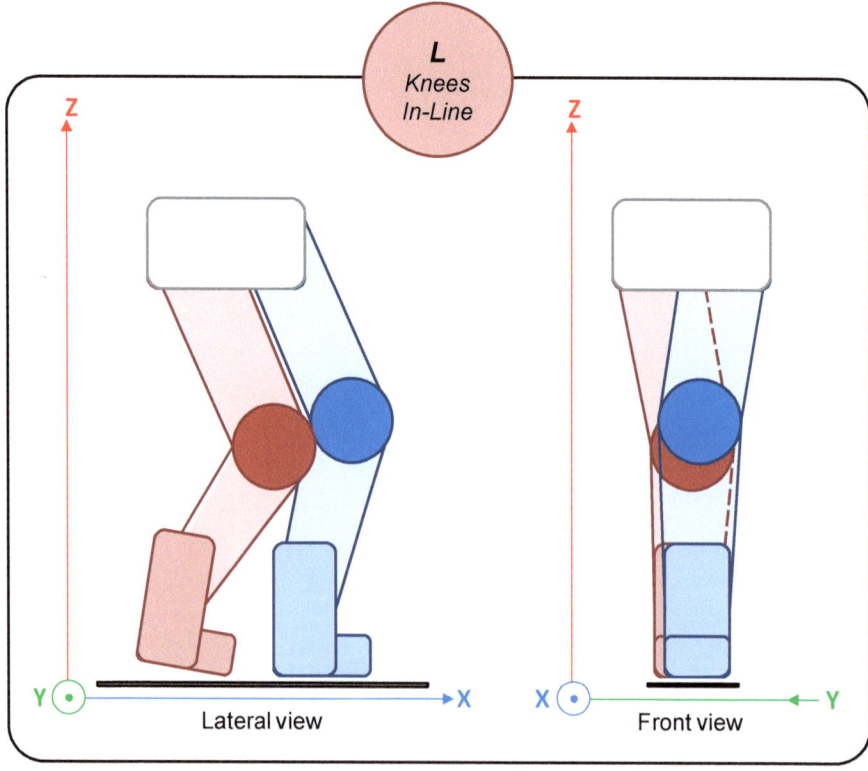

Free-Heel Boarding Techniques

In-line knee position

- The knees-**T**ogether position (T) in which:

    - The back heel will be lifted up significantly.

    - The back knee will come forward, on the side of the front knee.

    - The space between both knees is limited, a few centimeters or touching each other.

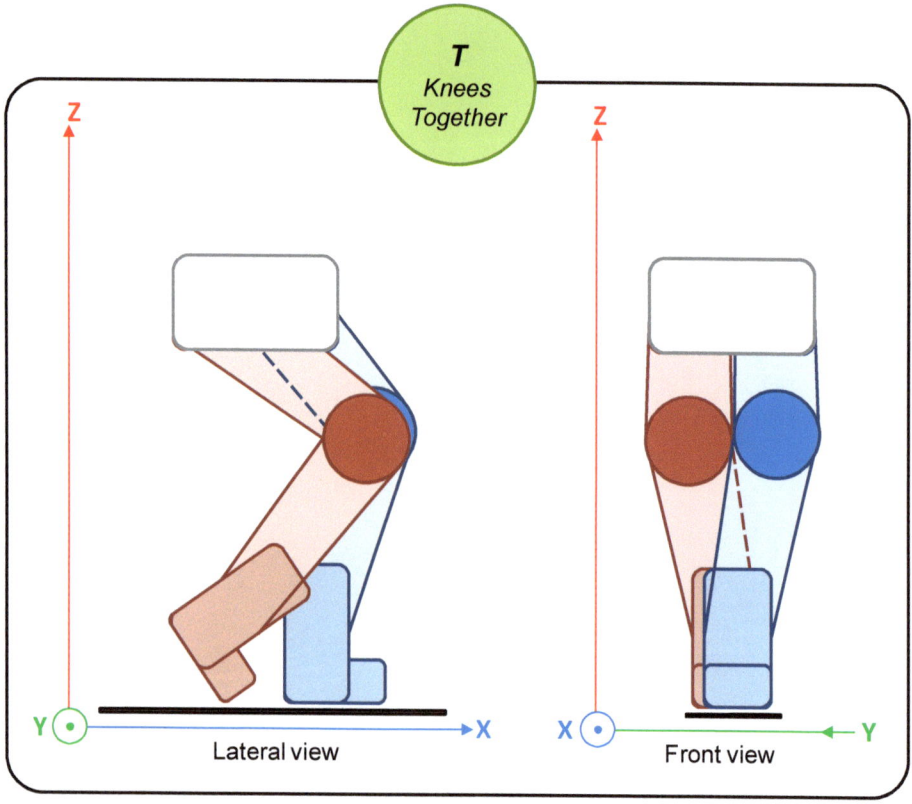

Free-Heel Boarding Techniques

Knees-together position

- The **F**ree position (F) in which:

    - The back heel will be slightly lift up, with the ability to go up or down significantly around this median position.

    - The back knee will come forward, but less than in the aforementioned position T.

    - The space between the knees will be quite significant (more than 10 centimeters) to allow for wide movements of the back knee.

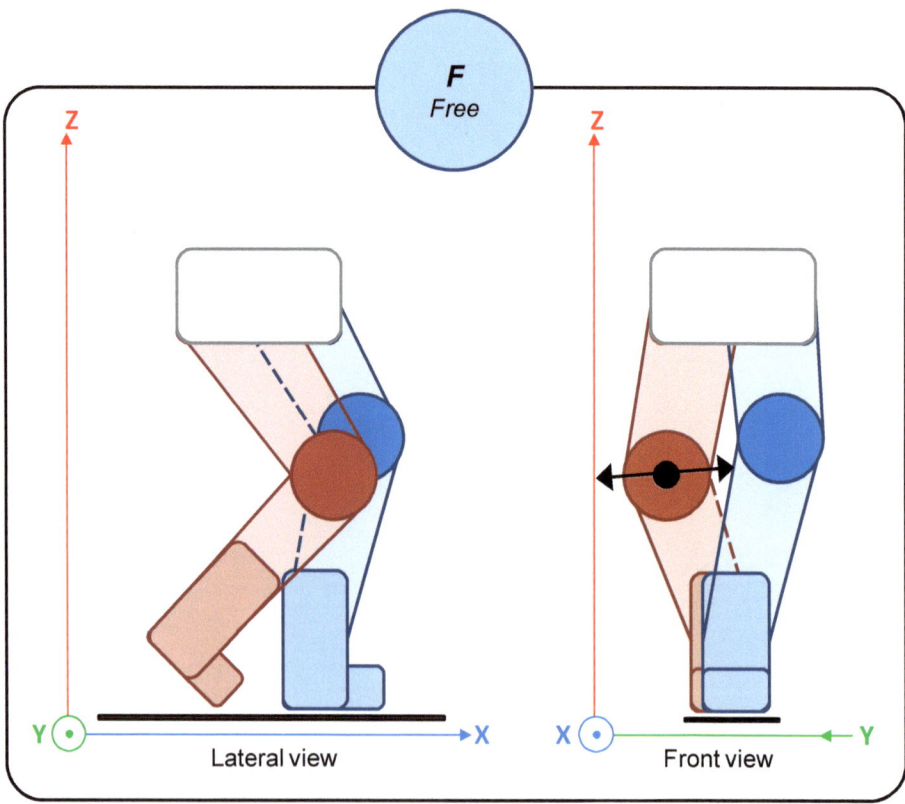

Free-Heel Boarding Techniques

Movements of the back knee in the free position

These three major riding stances are linked to a different set of turns. However, they are all part of free-heel boarding, and you can go through all three stances on one single run down depending on the terrain variations.

The positions L and T are linked to a mostly symmetrical riding style, whereas the position F will be a starting point for more efficiency and creativity with significantly asymmetrical turns.

Riding in the inline knee position (L) will remind you of skwalling. Most skwal technique can be applied to free-heeling with a slight variation. Riding in the knees-together position (T) will, in some ways, remind you of monoskiing, and that is, indeed, an efficient position usually combined with significant pole-use. This position allows you to drive the board through the knees in a monoski-like attitude. Riding in the free position (F), named as such because of the greater use of the back free heel, will remind you more of the Telemark turn (on one side).

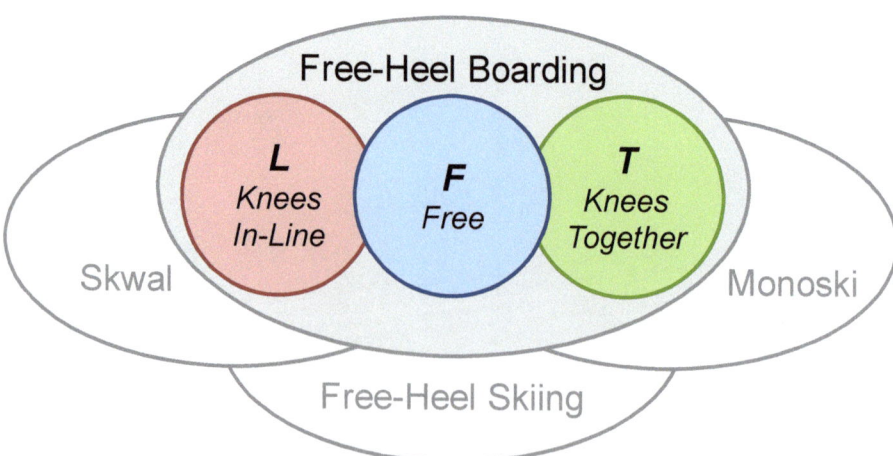

Free-heel boarding can benefit from blending the techniques of other sports, such as skwalling, monoskiing or Telemark skiing. It will also have a core of purely specific techniques (especially when riding in the F position).

Movement

Basics of skiing mechanics

When examining a turn on snow, it is always useful to start with the basics of mechanics. In *The Inner Glide*, Patrick Thias Balmain studies the basics of mechanics and how they apply to turning and carving on snow. From a mechanical perspective, Balmain's approach focuses mainly on the connection of the boarder with the ground. He also takes human psychology into account in his approach, and includes the sport of skiing in a much wider philosophical journey.

This is a book worth reading, regardless of which type of equipment you are skiing on. In this book, alpine skiing, snowboarding and skwalling are discussed in detail. Here, I will base my approach mainly on the mechanisms of gliding as described in *The Inner Glide*, but I will also consider the case of a free-heel board.

I should, therefore, remind you of some basic principles of gliding over snow as described in *The Inner Glide*.

When facing the fall line:

- If your weight is projected on the front of the board, the heavy will pull the light, and the board follows the fall line.
- If your weight is projected on the back of the board, the heavy has a tendency to lead the light, and the board will turn away from the fall line.

When going across the slope with the board flat:

- If the weight of the boarder is projected on the front of the board, the front of the board, which is heavier, will lead.

- If the weight of the boarder is projected on the back of the board, the back of the board will lead down the slope.

The body, therefore, does not need to be rotated to change direction.

While engaged in a sideslip down a steep slope:

- If you remain centered over the feet while braking (by increasing the degree of edge on the snow), the board will go down perpendicular to the fall line.

- Shifting the weight to the front when braking will intensify the braking on the front of the board, causing the back of the board to go down faster.

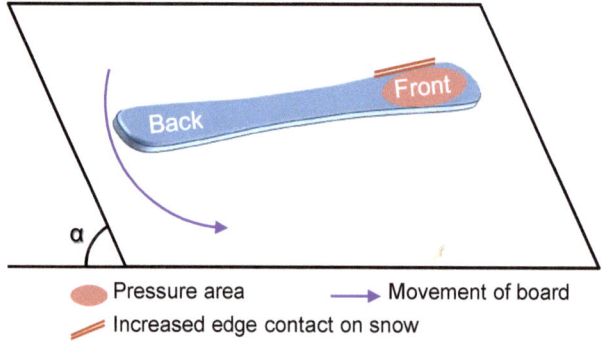

- Shifting the weight to the back when braking will intensify the braking on the back of the board, causing the front of the board to go down faster.

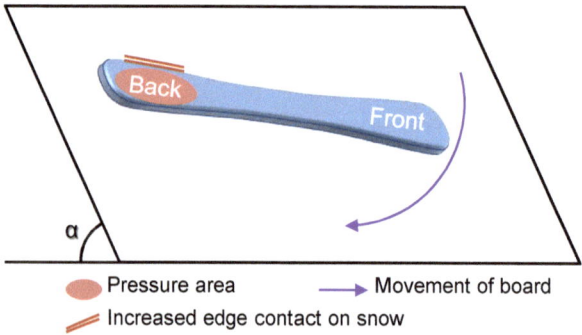

These basic gliding mechanics show that any board's course over snow can be controlled through managing the placement of your weight on the board. Because the feet are the sole interface between you and your board, mastering exactly where to put your weight on the soles of the feet is key to staying centered and gliding efficiently.

You psychologically focus on what really makes the board turn (your center of gravity and the projection of it on the soles of the feet) rather than on peripheral movements of arms, torso, legs, or knees. As Balmain says, you psychologically place yourself in *the axis that causes the wheel to turn* – your center of gravity is the center of movement.

Skidding on a free-heel board

Skidding

Whatever stance you are in (L, T or F), the aforementioned basics of mechanics still apply in the same way. Side-slipping and skidding turns are engaged and controlled by applying weight on the front or the back of the board. The angle of the edge on the slope is, among other things, controlled through the knees. Therefore, the stance you will adopt may vary depending on the difficulty of terrain on which you want to perform this type of turn.

For example, the T-stance (knees together) initiates powerful turns through the knees. This will be quite efficient for hard snow and medium-radius turns.

In the F-stance, the free back knee enables you to make quick variations of the edge angle on the snow; this can be useful if you need to perform a lot of short-radius turns.

Quick turns

It is possible to perform a series of extremely quick, skidded turns. To do that, you will mainly use rapid movements of the rear leg to change the direction of the board. This is only possible in a full F-stance. Quick turns are very useful for mastering bumps, avoiding others on a crowded slope, navigating narrow paths and catwalks, etc

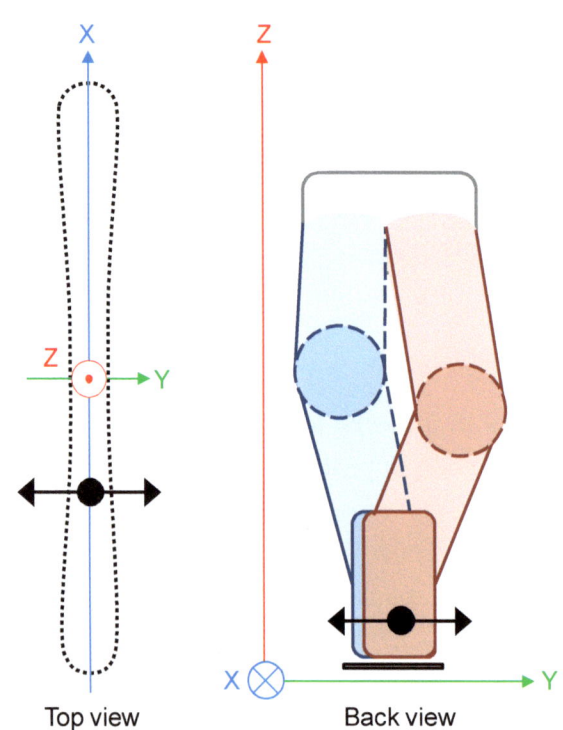

Top view   Back view

Drifting

Drifting is the action of *breaking* a carved turn so that it ends with a skidded turn, eventually into a full sideslip. This can be done for multiple reasons: shortening the radius of turn; preparing to stop at the end of the slope; or controlling speed while relaxing the legs and/or emergency stops.

In the F-stance, initiating the drift turn is done through the back leg and the free knee:

- More weight is put on the back leg;

- The knee is further directed to the center of the turn to increase the edge angle.

It shall be noted that the knee is not pulled towards the center of the turn when the weight is simultaneously put on the rear leg.

This approach may vary significantly if you are using a stiff board with sharply tuned edges for high-performance carving. This is particularly beneficial for carving, as it prevents the board from drifting. However, you will need to be able to drift with this type of free-heel board, simply so you can stop at the end of the slope. In this case, the above technique might be very difficult to apply. To allow for drifting, you need to first "extract" the back of the board from the carved trajectory. Drifting is initiated by putting your weight forward. The back knee will help in lifting the back of the board and extracting it from the rail (the track formed in the snow by the edge). Then, you rise, put your weight back and perform a typical drift.

Driving the turn: the figure-8 movement

To drive a carved turn, apply your weight laterally onto an edge – first on the front of the board; then, staying on that edge, your weight is progressively placed backward to the back of the board.

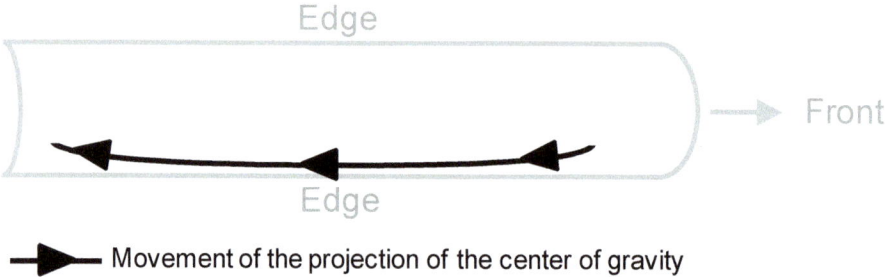

Movement of the projection of the center of gravity

To go into the next turn, your weight shifts to the front of the board on the other edge. Your center of gravity passes over the central position.

The trajectory of the projection of mass beneath the feet has the shape of the figure 8, as described by Balmain in *The Inner Glide*.

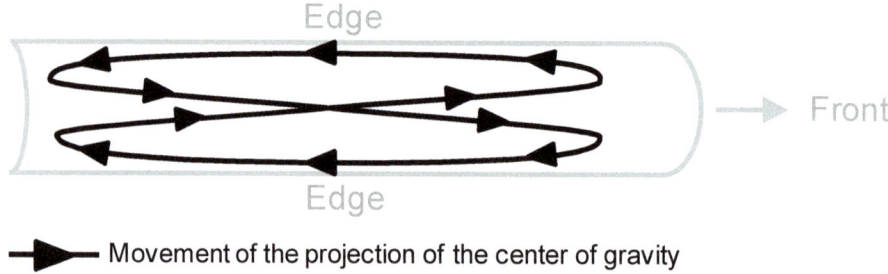

Movement of the projection of the center of gravity

During this transition, contact with the Earth has to be maintained. Otherwise, you would be making a sort of micro-jump turn by releasing the pressure on the board rather than driving the board through its natural rotation on snow. This notably implies permanent contact on the center of the feet in addition to shifting the weight onto one of their sides.

The figure-8-shaped lateral movement is also combined with a similar vertical movement. Center of gravity follows a figure-8-shaped movement in a vertical plan. This movement facilitates the shift of your weight from front to back and vice-versa. You are, in fact, engaging in a double-8-shaped movement.

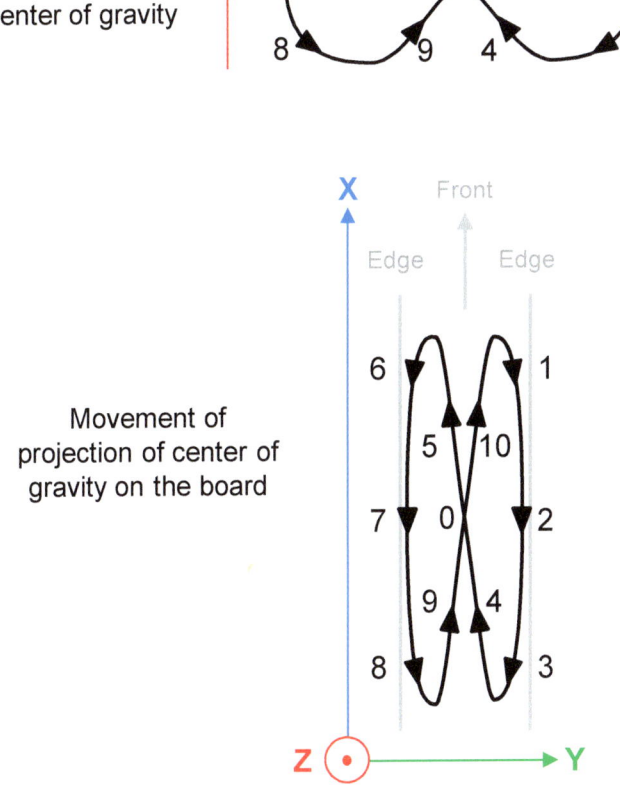

Free-Heel Boarding Techniques

The figure-8 movement on a free-heel board

Once again, whatever stance you are in, principles for riding a board still apply in the same way. What is really changing is the surface of your feet in contact with the board (and therefore the Earth) depending on your stance.

One of the major specifics of free-heel boarding is that the surface of contact between you and the Earth is not the entire soles of your feet. As the heels lift up, the contact sometimes can only be made through points 1 and 6. The projection of weight will be

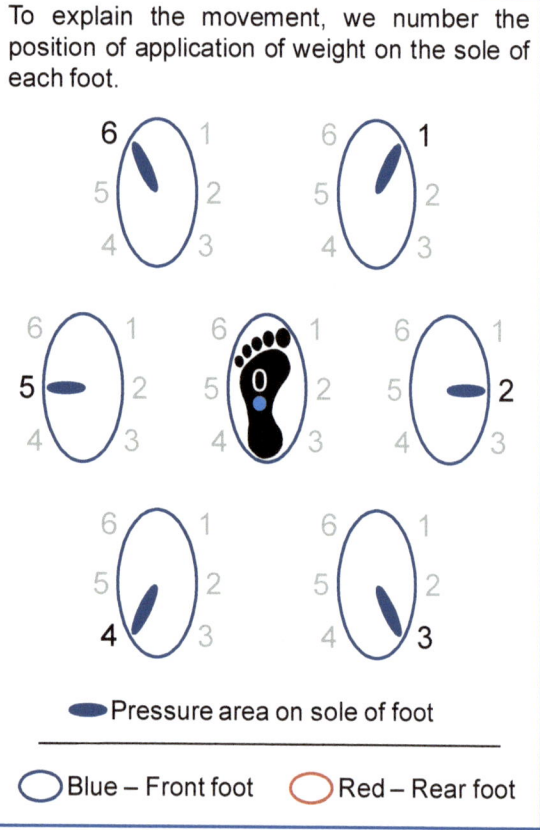

limited to these points. It will not be on the whole surface between 0 and 1, or 0 and 6.

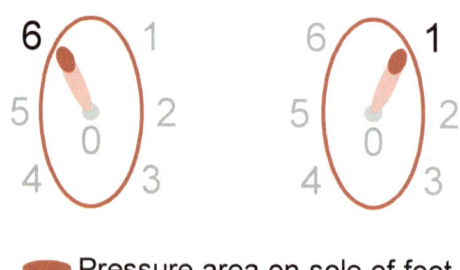

We will review in this section how the figure-8-shaped movement can be adapted to each particular stance that can be used in free-heel boarding.

In the T stance (knees together), the figure-8 movement will take the following shape:

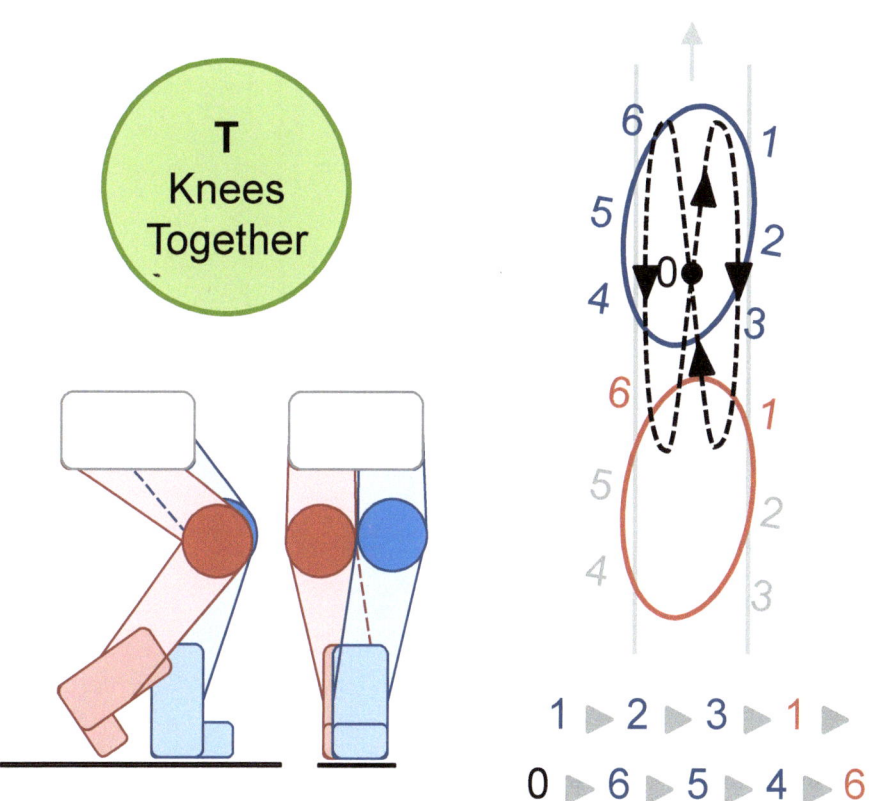

In the L stance (knees in line), the figure eight movement will take the following shape:

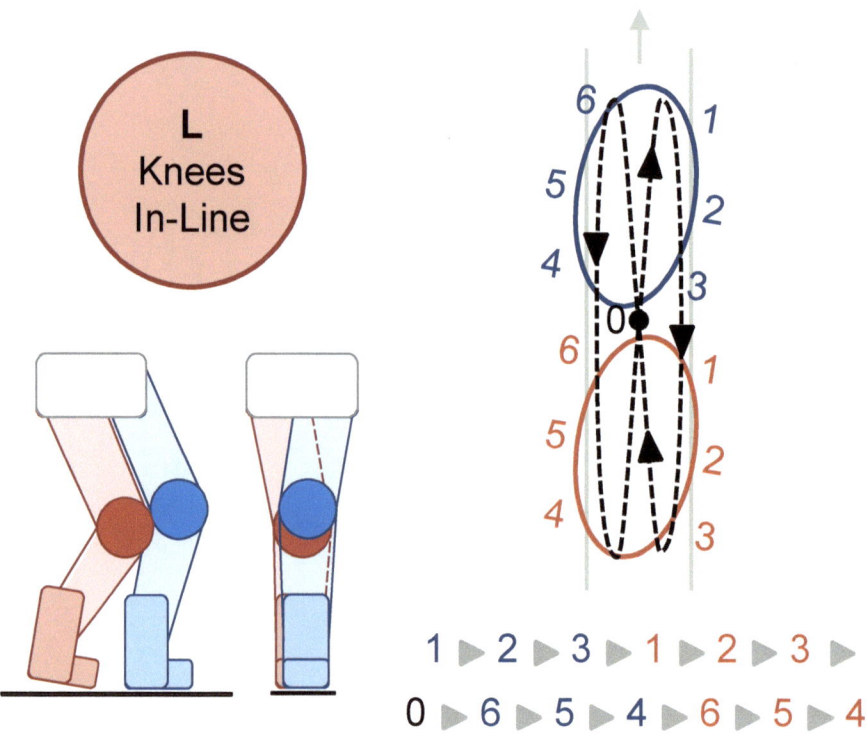

Because your heel is free when your weight is forward, there is in fact a limited loss of contact between the heel of the back boot and the board.

In the main F stance (free knee), the figure 8 movement will take the following shape:

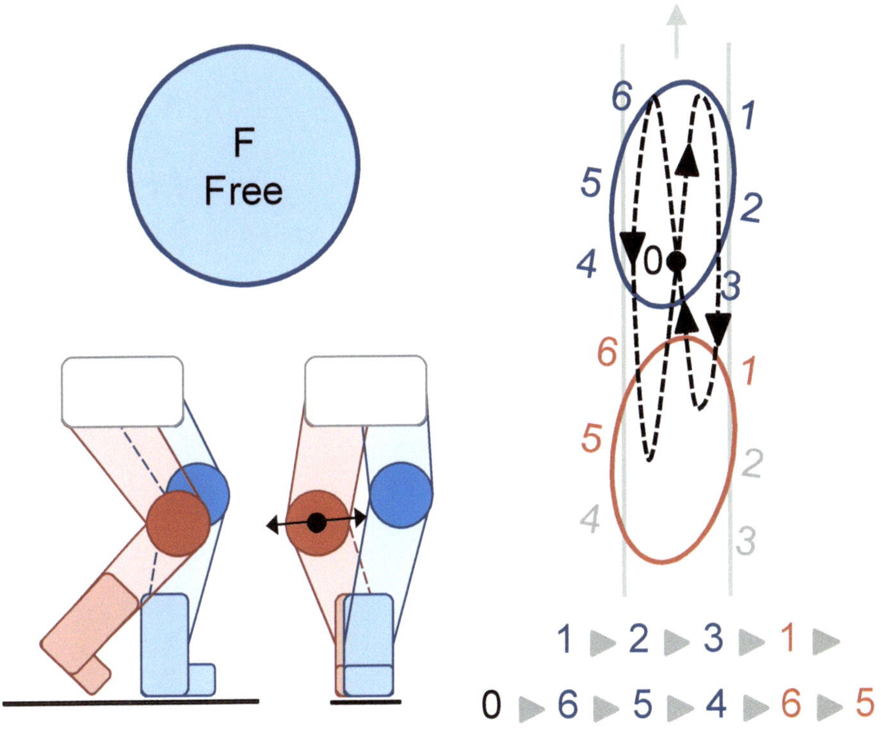

With this stance, the pressure will be applied a bit more back on the rear foot when using the left edge (regular stance). This is required to make more use of this edge through the back leg, because the front of the rear foot is closer to the center of the board, but not as close to the edge. A subtle pressure on the big toe and the big toe mound can be applied between position 6 and 5 as the back heel remains lifted up.

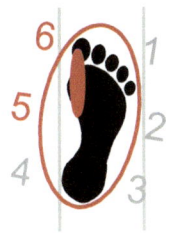

In the F stance, the movement can be slightly asymmetric – even to the point that is a mix between the L and F stance.

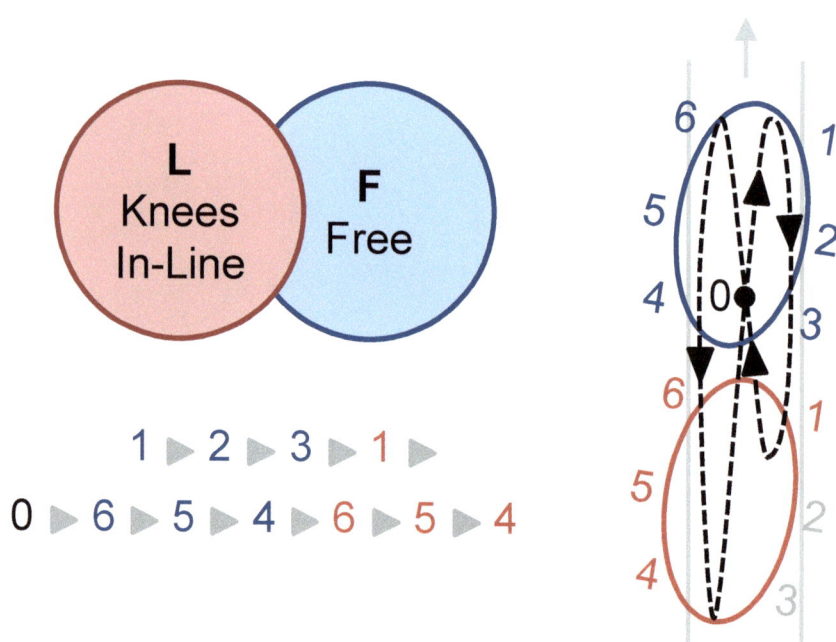

Jump turns

The jump turn fundamentally differs from the previous techniques that rely on the basics of board-to-snow mechanics. On the contrary, it is based on temporarily and voluntarily losing contact with the snow – a turn in the air.

Free-heel boards will allow for that, thanks to the ease of the flexion-extension movement and the use of poles. However, the free-heel gear also raises a few issues in comparison to other gear.

First, because the board is generally long (in comparison to other boards or even today's skis), this means that to turn it, you will need to produce more rotational force than with other gear. Once the rotation has started, there will be a force couple applied by the board on the legs. You then need to produce a counteracting rotational force to stop the rotation.

Second, the free heels allow forward and backward inclination of the board (i.e. the tip higher than the tail or the opposite). This is done in order to land all of the board at once and not its tail or tip first.

Third, the free-heel board provides great front-back equilibrium, but not much lateral equilibrium. When landing the jumped turn, the board might be perpendicular to (or at least not aligned with) the fall line – the worst position for keeping balance.

A jump turn can, however, be useful. So, how can these characteristics of the free-heel board be addressed to secure a safe and efficient jump turn?

- **Initiating rotation**: A pole plant can be used to help initiate the rotation. Plant the pole forward, and, when extending to start the jump turn, pull on the pole while rotating your hips around it.

- **Managing and stopping rotation:** If the rotation needs to be stopped earlier, you can quickly bend and stretch toward the snow to choose when to stop the rotation and force the board to land.

- **Managing the inclination of board in the air**: Both heels can be managed independently to influence the inclination of the board. This is just a matter of practicing to get the right feel for having a horizontal board when practicing jump turns.

- **Dealing with lateral equilibrium when landing perpendicular to the fall line:** In these circumstances, the hands will be well away from each other, and the poles will provide the wingspan to compensate for unbalanced landings.

Carving low

On any board, there are two major ways to carve and lean: either lean naturally as the consequence of a carved turn at significant speed; or by forcing lateral leaning from the beginning of the turn.

For the first kind of turn, it is just a consequence of the carved turn as previously discussed. If the movement is correctly performed and the speed is sufficient, you will get closer to the snow. Then, the hand can be stretched out in the direction of the interior of the turn to touch the snow.

Carved turn

It is also possible to force the board into hard-carving from the beginning of the turn, through the push-pull technique. Free-heel boards are perfect

Free-Heel Boarding Techniques

for this because of their considerable vertical flexion-extension capabilities. The point is just to turn this *vertical* capability into a *horizontal* one (aligned with the surface of the slope). The push-pull technique provides an answer for this.

It must be noted that the push-pull technique, as it does not permit maintaining a constant pressure on the board throughout the turn, is not an efficient technique for all conditions and all speeds. However, it can be quite pleasurable to use and is therefore worth mentioning for that reason alone.

Because the push-pull technique is mostly inherited from alpine snowboarding, I will allow myself, just this once, to speak of *frontside* and *backside* turns.

To perform these kinds of low carved turns, enter into a very low position before initiating the turn. Finger tips can touch the snow at this point.

Initiating a push-pull carved turn

The weight is on the front of the board. Then, when the board is still perpendicular to the fall line (or just a bit in the direction of the fall line), you:

- Lean in the direction of the fall line, laying your forearm in the snow as far down as you can. (The other hand can also touch the snow by passing it in front of the body; if not, the hand on the outside of the turn should be kept very close to the body. Placing it on the front knee is another possible option.)

- Pull the knee in the direction of the turn:
    - Don't overdo it if you're turning in the frontside direction.
    - For a backside turn, your rear leg will clearly touch and press on the front one.

- Strongly push with both legs.

As soon as the board passes the fall line, it is already time to pull back on the legs. The weight will then have shifted to the back of the board. Your legs must be flexible enough to allow the board to come back under your body and make the transition into the next turn.

Transitioning between turns is fast; in fact, the end of a turn is the start of the next one. The secret of a good *backside* turn lies in a perfect preceding *frontside* turn, and the other way round. When transitioning into the next turn, keep the leg compression obtained from the *pull* phase of the previous turn as the board passes *under* you, so you can put your weight forward and initiate the next turn. During the transition, the board and the snow remain in contact.

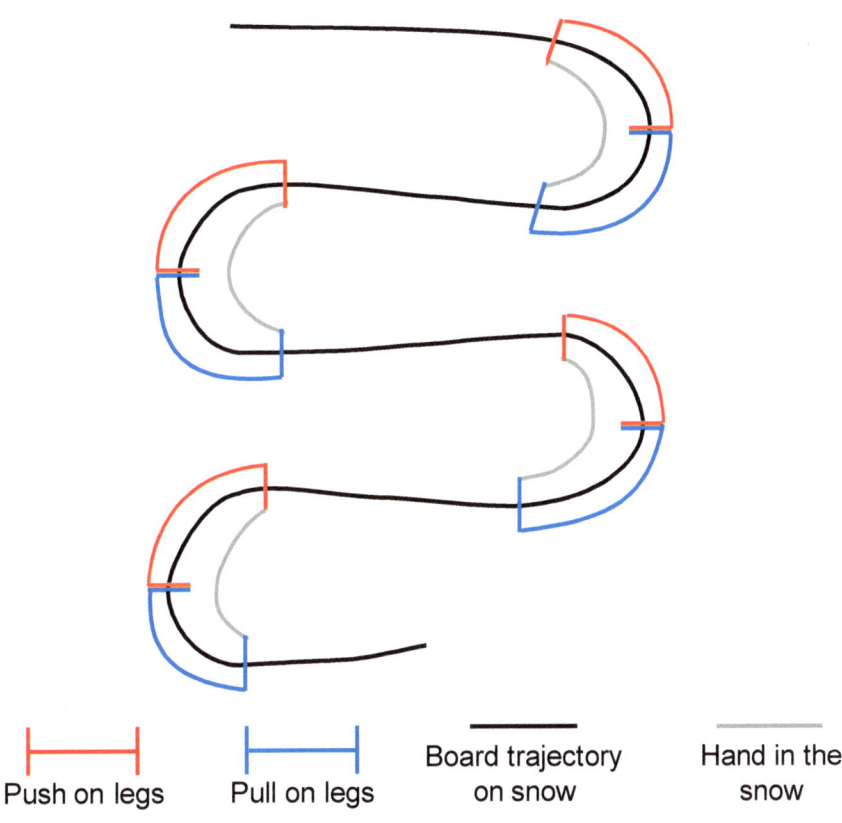

Be extremely careful of other skiers while carving low on the slopes. Because free-heel boarding has a front-facing stance, it is very easy to manage any traffic on the slope, as you are in the direction of the flow. While carving, you are making U-turns on the slope, with very limited visibility while your head is close to the snow. These are perfect conditions for crashing into someone who is not anticipating this kind of trajectory! So, wait for a clear slope to practice extreme carving safely.

Jumping

On a free-heel board, the Telemark position is permanent. It just needs to be used to land jumps (see position below). This also means that jumps can be done anywhere. Whatever happens on the slope, if you need to jump over a mogul, or if a bump kicks you up in the air, you are already in the most stable position possible for landing.

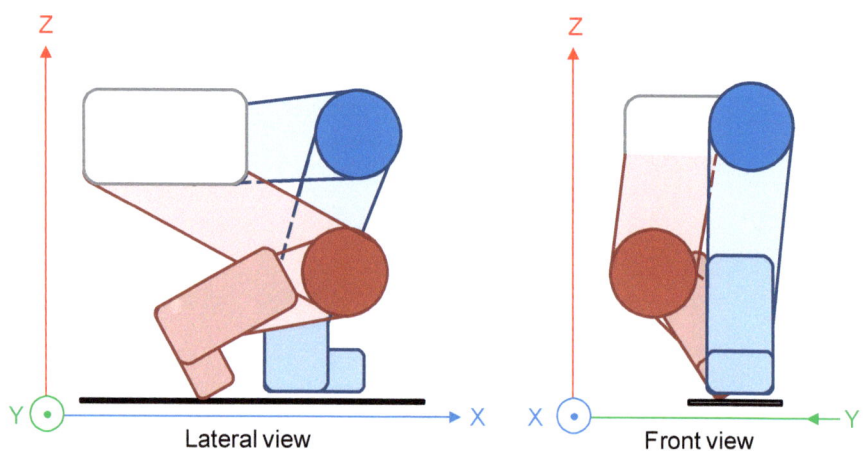

Snow conditions

Besides groomed slopes, there are several kinds of terrain through which you have to go. As in any downhill snow sport, there are a few tips to know to help you go through all conditions with ease.

Powder

Skiing in powder is three-dimensional skiing, which makes it differ from all other types of terrain, which are mostly two-dimensional (or partially three-dimensional if you include some jump turns).

In powder, first you need to float rather than sink. As previously discussed, the free-heel setup allows for riding long boards while keeping optimum maneuverability. With boards over 190cm, even if they are relatively narrow and without a rocker, there are already some good floating capabilities that can be achieved with a little speed. Once the minimal speed is reached, the three-dimensional riding starts. Then, you need to have a trajectory of up and down in the snow, caused by the weighting and unweighting of the board. It will be easiest to turn on the top of this trajectory. These are the basics of powder riding, whatever the board(s) you are on.

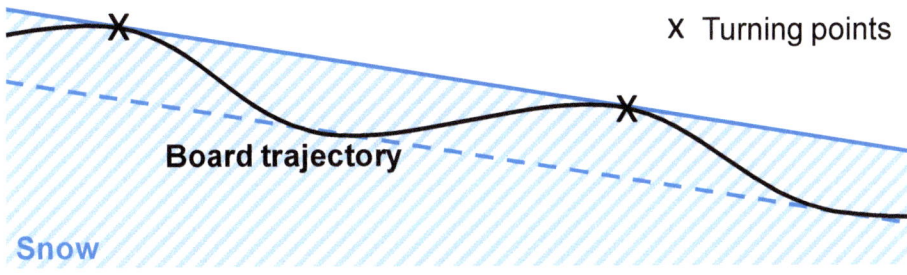

What is interesting with a free-heel board is that the front/back inclination of the board can be easily controlled autonomously from the weighting of the board. Pulling the rear foot and pushing on the front one, the board nose goes down into the snow. Pulling the front foot and pushing on the rear one, the board goes up. There's no need to push or pull the board vigorously; it is a very gentle movement. If combined with good rhythm with some weighting and unweighting movement, the board can be managed very easily in powder.

It is so easy to control the board in this three-dimensional environment that the up and down trajectory can be amplified. The rebound will then be fully exploited, so that the upper part of the trajectory (the *bell*) is done outside of the snow. It will leave a repeating, discontinuous signature in powder.

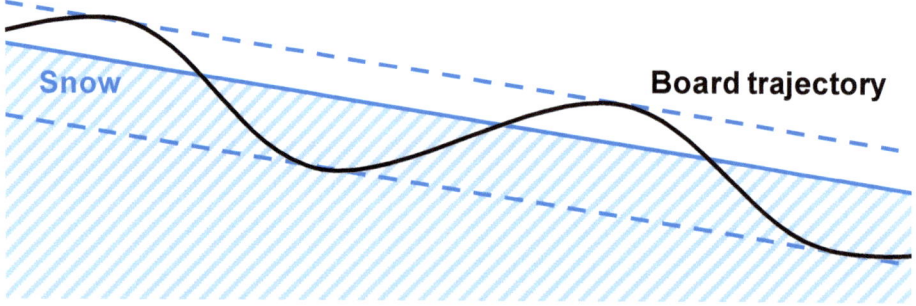

Free-heel boards consequently excel in powder due to this additional axis of maneuverability that cannot be managed in the same way on any other skiing sport board.

Crud

In crud, you will have to position your weight towards the back of the board, on your back leg. However, the heel is still up. The weight is therefore applied to the board through the front of the rear foot. The front leg is used to absorb terrain variation, and lift the board over the snow when need be. Free-heel boarding lets your board float over snow. As boards are relatively long, even with your weight backward, there is still a good length of board between the back foot and the tail to allow for efficient riding.

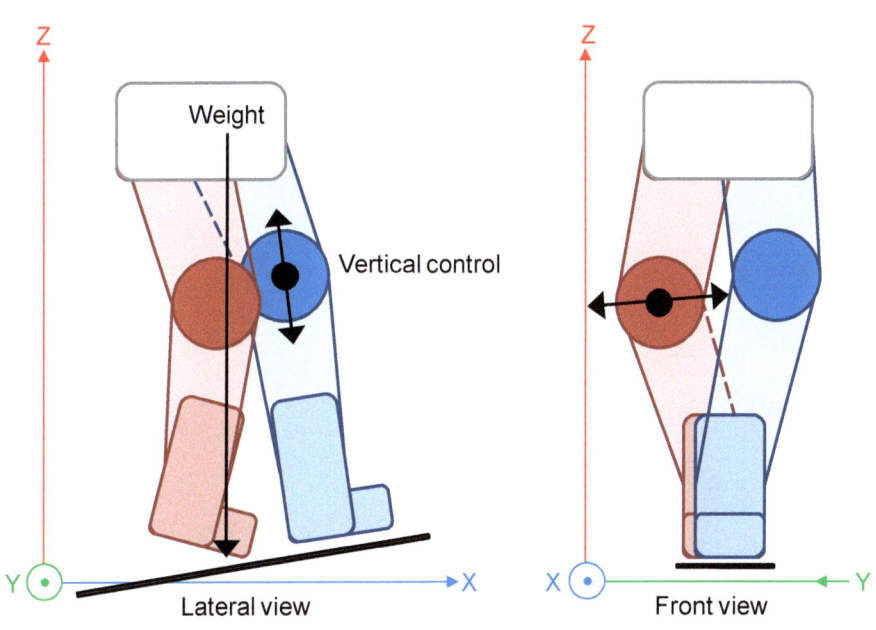

Slush

When the sun comes into the game with high temperatures, or, even more extreme, when rain also brings more unfrozen H_2O particles to ski on, there are all-new ways to ride!

Your weight needs to be put more on the back of the board. Due to its length, the board will still allow for some good carving even in wet snow.

In the worst slush and crud mix, a full backward position might be needed. The front leg will push on the rear spoiler of the front shoe. The front leg is used to keep the board above the snow. Knees will be side by side, because the front knee travels well backward. The lower legs, below the knees, are frozen into a position, making sure that the board can overcome any pack of snow. The absorption of vertical movements is accomplished by the thighs and knees. Indeed, it's not the most beautiful free-heel boarding style, but it enables you to overcome the worst kinds of snow conditions.

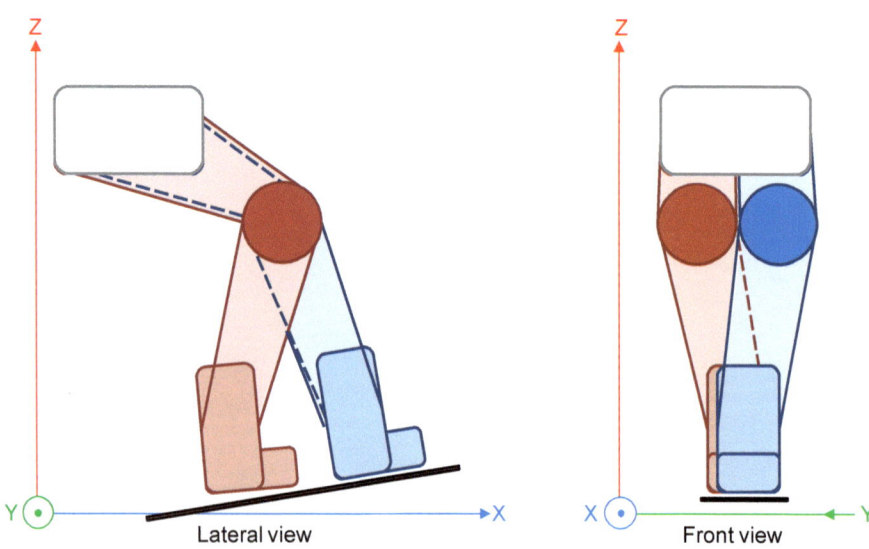

Free-Heel Boarding Techniques

Slush

Bumps / Moguls

Bumps are all about trajectory. You can turn on top of each one, go in the troughs, or ski at the mid-height of the bumps. Of course, shorter boards are easier to manage on such terrain.

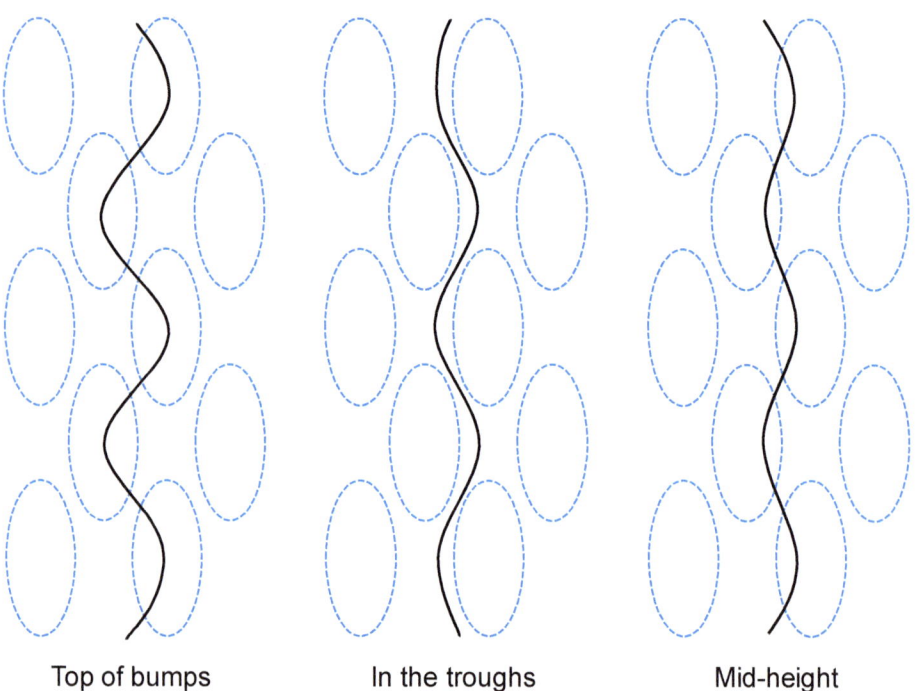

Top of bumps   In the troughs   Mid-height

The knees-together position (T) is one possible option. It is well-adapted for going through narrow bumps, relying on a good rhythm of pole plants and a monoski-like riding style. It will work for you whether you are skiing the top of the bumps or following the hollows.

Another approach, based on the free position (F), can also be considered for effective mogul technique. When entering into contact with the bump, you absorb the obstacle by going down (knees and heels are free to do so), and this significantly and abruptly reduces the speed. You have to go down when touching the bump, but don't go too early. Use your legs as shock-absorbers. After passing the top, try to keep the board in contact with the snow on the way down the bump rather than flying over it. Your center of gravity is more or less following a straight line. The free heels facilitate this through the three-dimensional movement capabilities they provide.

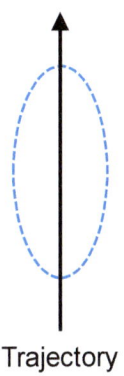

Trajectory from above

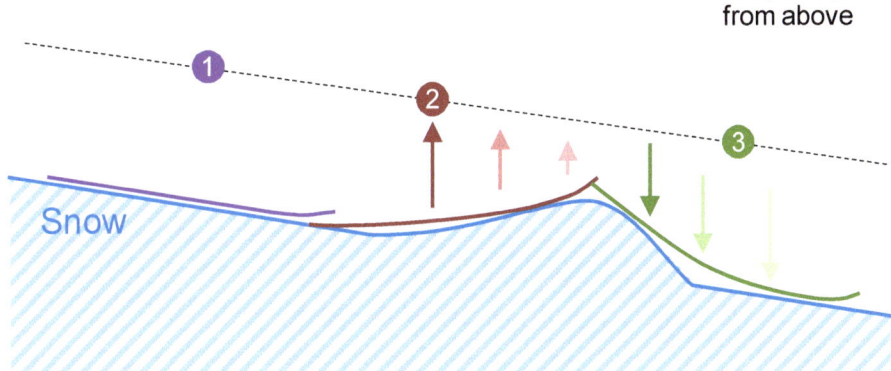

↑ Movement of legs / Pressure applied at different stages
✖ Center of gravity

Depending on the bumpiness of the terrain, the hardness of snow and the distance between the bumps, you can choose any technique and adapt the trajectory. This last technique is, however, important to master, so you can absorb unexpected terrain variations in conditions other than a field of bumps. It is also a fun way to go through bumps when the snow is still relatively soft, as it gives you the feeling that the bumps are splitting in two for you in front of the board.

The steeps

On steep slopes, it might be difficult to apply the common technique of the free-heel turn, because one of your objectives might be to control your speed during the turn.

One option is to rely on a specific turn based on the inline knee position (L). Before the turn, you lock into the inline knee position (regardless of the direction of the turn) with a low stance. Then, to initiate the turn, put your weight forward rapidly, and, at the same time, point the board in the direction of the fall line as the tail lifts up to ease the turn. As soon as the board is in the fall line (still with little speed except that provided by the turn initiation), you forcefully extend your legs to quickly finish the turn.

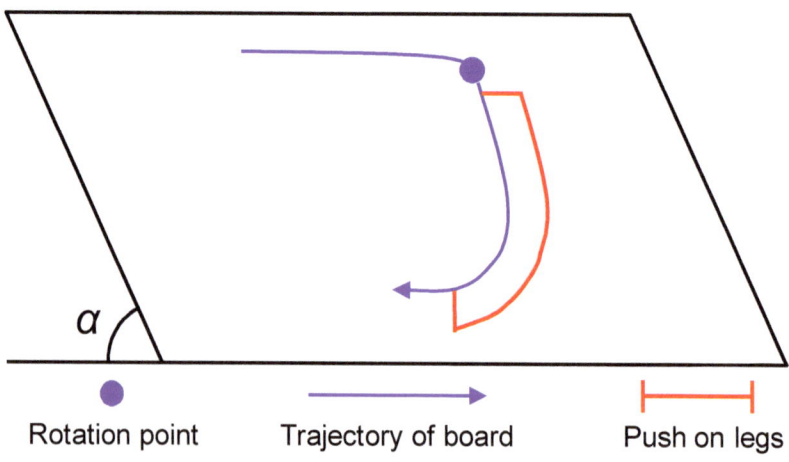

To make this turn, the free knee should not migrate away from the other knee. The turn initiation can only be performed well if both knees are kept together, so you can lift the tail of the board. The back knee should be kept behind the front knee during the whole turn. This turn is clearly borrowed from skwalling techniques.

The jump turn is another possible option for certain terrain, for example, the steeps. However losing contact with the snow and landing in the least-balanced position possible might not be the preferred option. To perform a jump turn on a steep slope with a free-heel board requires slightly different management of the board inclination in comparison to a flatter slope. The goal is not to keep the board horizontal all the way through the air but to keep it parallel to the slope.

Aesthetics and Free-Heel Boarding

What are aesthetics in skiing?

What are aesthetics in skiing?

That's a rather complicated question. I am not intending to write an essay about skiing aesthetics. I am certainly not qualified to do that! I will however try to provide a short definition anyway, to guide us in considering free-heel boarding aesthetics. I would define an aesthetic impression as an image provided by the ride that somehow touches peoples' minds in a way that evokes positive feelings. A positive value could be strength, purity, lightness … even some fragility.

I am not referring to *beauty,* as it would itself need to be defined and put in context. I prefer to refer to *positive values* that are shared by most of mankind.

For something to be valued, it also has to stand out in some way from the rest of the environment. To make a difference, either you are one of the best (and it's fairly obvious in comparison to the others) or you are simply different. Considering the current state of development of free-heel boarding, it's not that hard to be different from the vast majority of others skiers in the mountain. However, the level of efficiency must at least be comparable to other skiers to be worth considering in terms of *skiing style*. Otherwise, you're still climbing up the learning curve rather than working on improving aesthetics.

Telemarking is an interesting example to be considered for giving us some hints on aesthetics in skiing. Indeed, during its recent re-emergence, it has attracted a lot of people because of its aesthetic aspect. The genuflexion, when combined with superior skills in the descent, creates an incredible impression to non-free-heelers. This is not an ordinary body position in real life.

Descending a mountain efficiently in this position can seem theoretically impossible to anyone who is not accustomed to it. The linking of turns with the body laterally arched liked a C combined with skis and snow only touched by the toes seems like dancing. In this, we can see fragility and fluidity. Once spectators get accustomed to it, and as the sport became more widespread, the criteria for style became more refined.

The feeling of power and mastery of any snowsport can also be aesthetic. That's the kind of thing more often noticed from an outstanding performer in a competition or by skiers who safely demonstrate an outstanding level of performance and speed on the slopes.

To address aesthetics on a free-heel board, it would be impossible to provide a *how-to* methodology. This belongs to each boarder in the construction of his/her individual style. I would rather start from the set of positively inspiring values discussed above, and consider how they can radiate into free-heel boarding.

Ease of execution: the efficiency in doing what should be impossible

For most of those who have never seen a free-heel boarder and that practice neither skwal nor free-heel skiing, there is already a major psychological barrier to considering the possibility of free-heel boarding. Having both feet attached only by the toes to a single board in this position is something that most consider either dangerous or totally impossible. Seeing a free-heel boarder perfectly at ease on a slope is already shocking. However, this does not make it aesthetic by itself yet. But it can help convey such feelings.

Carving

So, a first critical point for bringing aesthetics into free-heel boarding is to give the impression that this is *easy* for the boarder. Even if the boarder is, in fact, working hard using a variety of muscles at this time, this impression of ease can be given by:

- The absence of wide movements: the arms are not moving in all directions to help with balance, and hips and the middle of the body are not going from side to side.

- The absence of poles (or if you have poles, you're not using them extensively and aligning them in the direction of the movement).

This ease of movement on snow becomes *outstanding* when demonstrated on terrain or in situations where there are few possible comparisons. For example, free-heel boarding gear clearly distinguishes itself in:

- Landing jumps in the Telemark position (truly unique on a board).

- Carving close to the snow (Only extreme carving on an alpine snowboard or skwal can be compared to free-heel carving.)

- Powder skiing (While other snowsports enable you to go in powder, free-heel boarding is distinguished by its powder style.)

Power

The image of power and strength is often linked to anything massive and fast.

The free-heel boarder dynamically conveys this image through:

- The front-facing position: the fall line is *the way* down
- The speed: thanks to the stability of long boards and their effective edge, a significant speed can safely be reached.
- Issues regarding passing over obstacles or potential obstacles (soft moguls or soft crud) can be overcome, and therefore, should not be considered as impediments to the boarder trajectory.

From a fully static perspective, the length of some boards (about two meters) is in itself impressive, as they are taller than every other board on the slopes by a few dozen centimeters (and taller than most boarders). But this is mostly visible at the bar terrace!

Front-facing

Aesthetics and Free-Heel Boarding

Fragility

An apparent fragility reinforces the impression of the ease of execution, as well as becoming something truly unique to see.

Free-heel boarding will convey this image through its specific stance:

- A back heel significantly lifting up: clearly showing that the point of contact with the board is extremely limited.

- A low stance: making the boarder appear *small* in comparison to the length of the board.

- Both heels lifting up on flat or well-groomed terrain.

Heels up !

Fluidity

Fluidity is about demonstrating a continuous and soft movement; it is purely related to the dynamics of skiing.

Free-heel boarders can work on this through:

- The substantial flexion-extension capability gives the impression of never having to brutally absorb any variation of terrain. Indeed, amplitude of movement can be used to transform a swift reaction into a kneeling one with fluidity.

- The excellent maneuverability in comparison to the length of the board makes for fast, short, soft turns that look like a snake crawling down the slope.

The poles can keep tempo to support this.

Conclusion

At first glance, there's indeed a bit of a paradox with free-heel boards. The combination of free-heel bindings and a single board creates an apparently odd-looking set-up.

But examining it more carefully, it opens a unique range of possibilities (of movements especially) that can be turned into an advantage in various snow conditions. All these possibilities can be used in unique and multifaceted free-heel boarding techniques, making the free-heel boarder perfectly at ease with all snow conditions and terrains.

You are not yet a free-heel boarder? Do you want to try it? Get good gear first (this might be the hardest part depending on your location)! A soft board is recommended for novices. Use adjustable poles. Put the same foot forward as you would on a snowboard or skwal. Helmet and goggles on, and here we go!

Bibliography

The Inner Glide, Patrick Thias Balmain, Destiny Books, 2007

Free-heel Skiing: Telemark and Parallel Techniques – Third edition, Paul Parker, The Mountaineers Books, 2001

Allen & Mike's Really Cool Telemark Tips, Allen O'Bannon and Mike Clelland, A Falcon Guide, 1998

www.free-heel-boarding.com

www.ingramcontent.com/pod-product-compliance
Lightning Source LLC
Chambersburg PA
CBHW042323150426
43192CB00001B/31